# COMMON GRACE

# COMMON GRACE

HOW TO BE A PERSON
*and*
OTHER SPIRITUAL MATTERS

ANTHONY B. ROBINSON

SASQUATCH BOOKS
SEATTLE

Printed in Canada
Published by Sasquatch Books
Distributed by Publishers Group West
15 14 13 12 11 10 09 08 07 06      9 8 7 6 5 4 3 2 1

Book design by Judith Stagnitto Abbate/Abbate Design
Jacket design by Judith Stagnitto Abbate/Abbate Design
Composition by Kate Basart/Union Pageworks
Cover photograph © Getty Images

Unless otherwise noted, all Bible quotations are taken from the New Revised Standard Version (NRSV).

Some chapters were previously published, in slightly different form, as listed below:
"On Grace" and "The General Dance" appeared in *Words for the Journey: Letters to our Teenagers About Faith and Life*, The Pilgrim Press, Cleveland, 2003.

"The Blessed Trial: On Being a Parent" appeared in *The Journal for Preachers*, Columbia Theological Seminary, Decatur, Georgia, 1990.

"Hyper-Parenting," "On Being a Grown-Up," "Grievance Gluttony," "Jesus and Darwin," "The Gay Divide," "Who Are Those Christians," and "In a Time of War," appeared in the *Seattle Post-Intelligencer*, Seattle, Washington, between 1998 and 2004. "Singing of Sex: Re-reading the Song of Solomon" appeared in *The Christian Century*, 2004.

Library of Congress Cataloging-in-Publication Data is available.

ISBN: 1-57061-460-1

SASQUATCH BOOKS
119 South Main Street, Suite 400 | Seattle, WA 98104 | 206/467-4300
www.sasquatchbooks.com | custserv@sasquatchbooks.com

*Dedicated to Linda, companion and friend,*

*"Through many dangers, toils, and snares we have already come . . ."*

# CONTENTS

## PART THREE: **ON SOCIETY**

# INTRODUCTION

I T IS STANDARD in theological study to distinguish between "special" and "common" grace. For Christians, special grace is mainly about Jesus Christ and what we can know of God through his life and teachings, death and resurrection. Common grace, on the other hand, focuses on what we can know of God, the Spirit, or a transcendent dimension through more ordinary means: an oak tree or an osprey, a father or a friend, dramas on stage as well as the unfolding drama of history, and all of life's daily challenges, disappointments, and triumphs. Hence, the title of this work, *Common Grace*, and its subject matter, experiences of goodness and mercy, morals and mystery, sorrow and suffering in daily life and living.

This is a book of essays divided into three parts. The first is mostly about matters of faith. I hope that these pieces will prove of interest and value to those who understand themselves as persons of faith, but also to those who identify with no particular faith or religion at all. In this section I reflect mostly on my own faith: how I experience it and what it means to me, as well as some of the questions I have asked and been asked as a pastor and teacher over the years.

The second section is about relationships and people in relationship. I write of my experience as a son and as a father, as a husband and as a friend. I ponder qualities that all such relationships have need of sooner or later, and usually sooner, namely forbearance and forgiveness. I include a piece about sex based on the Song of Solomon. I explore the role and place of fathers in their children's lives and in society. I ponder the way we mark the earthly end of relationships at death and how this has changed in my lifetime.

Section three includes essays on society and topics that relate to our own society. I begin with a piece on the ministry, "Notes of a Field-Based Scholar: A View of the Ministry," which conveys something of my understanding of the ordained ministry. After laying that modest foundation, I follow with some articles and essays on different questions and topics with which we struggle as a society, including leadership, pluralism, homosexuality, technology, postmodernism, war, and terrorism. Several of these pieces were first published elsewhere, but most are new for this collection. It is not my aim in this book to offer or claim a definitive word or conclusive perspective on these various topics. Rather I hope to get you to think along with me and to deepen our shared appreciation of the grace in common things as well as in ordinary living.

Throughout the text I cite various authors. Wherever possible I have tried to supply references so that readers who wish to may pursue these ideas and authors further. But preachers are people who collect words and thoughts like magnets collect metal filings. We scribble things down as we read or hear them and do not always get a source or citation. We participate, I guess you might say, in an oral tradition. In some instances, therefore, I have been unable to find a source or reference. Please accept my apologies.

I have been extremely fortunate to have people around me who thought I had something to say, whether in print or from a pulpit. They have graciously afforded me the opportunity to do so, and so have contributed to my growth as well as whatever modicum of wisdom I may have gained along the way. In this connection I am deeply grateful to the four congregations I have served as a pastor, to the various publishers of previous books I've written, to the *Christian Century* magazine, publisher of many of my articles, and to the *Seattle Post-Intelligencer*, which has carried my Op-Ed columns for nearly a decade now as well as occasional articles in its Sunday Focus section.

Especially I wish to thank the following individuals for their assistance in this project: my former colleague at Plymouth Church, Kristine Anderson Ostrem, who read a number of the essays in draft; and my two sons and daughter, each of whom read and commented helpfully on several essays. A special word of appreciation is due Gary Luke, editorial director at Sasquatch Books. It was Gary who invited me to put together such a book in the first place. When he proposed it, Gary suggested that I might write "secular sermons." I didn't let on at the time, or at least I don't think I did, but my immediate thought was, "I'm not sure I can do that, that is, write something sermonic that is drained of faith or God."

When I gave the first draft of the manuscript to Gary I did so with trepidation because it did include more on faith and religious experience than I thought he might have bargained for. When we met to go over it, Gary confessed that his initial reaction had indeed been, "This can't be, there's too much Bible, too much God." Then he said a wonderful thing, for which I am immensely grateful. "But we asked you to write in your own voice, and this is your authentic voice. This is who you are." Gary also said that when he got to the third section, in that first draft, he was actually disappointed that there wasn't more overt Bible and theology. I told him that he was a "quick convert." In the current social climate, where ultraconservative and ultraliberal versions of faith and theology vie for the headlines, I hope my approach may provide a modest alternative.

Finally, I thank my wife, Linda, for her support and her wisdom. It is to her I dedicate this book with love and gratitude for life shared and its common graces.

PART ONE

# ON FAITH

# I BELIEVE IN
# BELIEVING

THE CHRISTMAS OF 1996 was an unusual one for Seattle. It was a white Christmas. "Snow had fallen, snow on snow," as Christina Rossetti puts it in a poem that became the hymn "In the Bleak Midwinter." Usually temperate and mild, Seattle was buried beneath two feet of snow, the result of a succession of storms, the latest of which had brought snow through the night of December 28. Nevertheless, being the stubborn type, I decided to go ahead with morning services at our downtown church, regardless of the amount of snow. It turned out to be a good thing we did, not so much for the quality of my sermon but because before the service we discovered the flat roof over the sanctuary was about to rupture under the weight of wet snow. Already a waterfall cascaded down one interior wall of the sanctuary where a seam had ruptured. A couple of people, among them my eldest son, mounted the roof and began pushing the accumulation of wet snow over the side.

As the day went on, the snow turned to rain and ate away at the accumulation on the streets. The warming weather meant that the plane twenty of us were scheduled to board that night at Seattle-Tacoma International Airport could take off. Somehow we all managed to get to the airport that night. Our flight, scheduled for a 9:30 P.M. departure, eventually departed close to 1:00 A.M. We were off, a youth group and three adults, to Nicaragua to spend ten days with the congregation of our sister church.

That morning at church one of the few members who showed up for services slipped a slender book into my hands, a Christmas gift. It was the second volume of Frederick Buechner's autobiography, *Now and Then*. Buechner is both a writer and a minister. I had a read a lot of Buechner ten years earlier and found both solace and encouragement in his explorations of faith and its meaning. But on that snowy morning, I was ambivalent about the gift. Several years before, I had decided that I had read enough of Buechner, that I had learned all I could from him and should move on. Despite that ambivalence, on impulse I tucked the new book into my bag that afternoon as we packed. I seldom travel anywhere without at least several books. But in my haste, it turned out that Buechner's *Now and Then* was the only book I had packed.

The group traveling to Nicaragua included my two sons; the youngest was still in high school, and the eldest had graduated from college the previous June. My eldest son had been an increasing source of concern for my wife, Linda, and me. We sensed something was not right, but we didn't know exactly what. His mood shifted rapidly. He seemed to have difficulty thinking in ways that we thought of as realistic or logical. In many agonized late-night conversations with my wife about him, I generally took the view that we had to let go and let him try his wings, while Linda thought that might be the worst thing we could do. At some level, of course, both of us knew we had little choice in the matter. We did not control him or his decisions. Fluent in Spanish, he planned to accompany the group from our church, and then continue traveling on his own in Central and South America throughout the winter and spring. Needless to say, his plans caused us considerable anxiety.

During the weeks leading up to Christmas our eldest son seldom seemed to sleep, at least at night, and was alternately exuberant and irritable. We arrived in Managua on New Year's Eve and were met by thirty beaming and excited young Nicaraguans, the youth group of our sister church. Bring together fifty high-school kids at the holidays and you pretty much get a continuous party. The school bus in which we all traveled, Nicaraguans and Americans, reverberated with shouts and conversation, laughter and loud music—pure torture for someone of more introverted tendencies like myself, who was, moreover, recovering from the rigors of being a pastor at Christmas and its seemingly endless succession of services and events.

The rapid change of climate, from winter snows to tropical sunshine, the fusion and excitement of the kids, the exotic sights of a profoundly different culture than our own, as well as the change of two time zones had one other result—we were sleepless in Managua. For a succession of nights our group was up until 3:00 A.M., to be roused out of bed at 7:30 for an 8:00 breakfast and the day ahead. But my eldest son did not, I think, sleep at all even during those short nights. It wasn't long before he began to show signs, which I recognized with growing apprehension, of the onset of a psychotic episode. More than anything, it was the unusual and exaggerated character of his body movements that was the tip-off. Later, after he and I had returned to the United States, sometime after the larger group made their scheduled return, he was diagnosed with manic-depressive illness. It made sense, and explained the manic highs and depressive lows of his rapidly shifting moods. It also fit his erratic sleeping and eating patterns; we learned after his diagnosis that prolonged sleeplessness can trigger a manic episode.

I knew in my gut that he was ill—desperately ill—but the other adults on the trip to Nicaragua weren't convinced. They agreed he was acting odd and sometimes disruptive but chalked it up as typical and harmless behavior of a young man in his carefree early twenties, who was neither fish nor fowl, neither a high-school student like the others nor quite fully adult, effusive one minute but difficult and perplexing the next. I hoped they were right, but somehow I knew they weren't. I saw a train wreck coming, and for the first and only time in my life I found myself weeping uncontrollably when I was alone. Hoping against hope that my fellow, more optimistic adult chaperones were correct in their assessment of my son, we boarded a rickety old DC-3, with duct tape on its wings, bound for Nicaragua's more remote eastern coast, where we were to spend several days. There he only grew worse. In time, my single agenda, besides doing what I could to keep him safe, became getting back on a plane to Managua and finding a doctor. As the east coast was to be his jump-off point for his solo travels, his return to Managua was hardly assured.

One afternoon during our stay on the east coast, the group was visiting some sort of school. My son and I sat and walked outside, since he had become unable or unwilling to be in any room or enclosed space for long. He was simultaneously sleepy and agitated, and in a mood to challenge his minister father. All young adults, I'm sure, have some things to say that are difficult for their parents to hear. A father who is a clergyman presents an unusually large target. He had lots to say that day, much of it not terribly coherent, but one thing came through loud and clear and pierced to my heart: "You've got to believe," he said, "you just have to believe." It seemed both a challenge and a plea. What he meant exactly, I'm not certain, nor do I think he even tried to spell it out. What I heard was both an indictment of my own tepid faith and an invitation, in the midst of our shared crisis and vulnerability, to trust. Even though I knew he was very ill, I believed he was telling me an important truth, maybe the one truth I needed to hear.

In the few moments of downtime I did have during our increasingly perilous journey, I had started reading Buechner's book, the second volume of his autobiography. It recounted his years at Union Theological Seminary in New York, where I had gone to school myself two decades after Buechner, and later his early ministry as a chaplain and preacher at Philips-Exeter Academy. Reading his book in snippets provided a welcome escape from the ongoing stress of our situation. Among the stories Buechner tells in *Now and Then* is one about his encounter with Agnes Sanford, a Christian healer. For a seminary-educated, Presbyterian-ordained minister to seek out someone like Agnes Sanford was, well, at the very least unexpected and perhaps even scandalous. Sanford did not operate within the cautious and rational versions of faith that tended to be the habitat of persons like Buechner or myself. That he sought out Sanford reflected Buechner's own longing for something more than the highly intellectualized, if ethical, faith of our shared tradition. But faith healing?

During his conference with Sanford, Buechner recounts that "The most vivid image she presented was of Jesus standing in church services all over Christendom with his hands tied behind his back and unable to do any mighty works because the ministers who led the services either didn't expect him to do them or didn't dare ask him to do them for fear that he wouldn't or couldn't and that their own faith and the faith of their congregations would be threatened as a result." Buechner goes on to say, "I immediately recognized my kinship with those ministers." And I recognized my kinship with Buechner.

My son's challenge, "You've got to believe," and Sanford's challenge, mediated through Buechner, seemed one and the same. I saw how timid and guarded my own faith was. I heard anew, even as my world broke asunder, the invitation to a raw and naked trust in the power of God to uphold us, and to heal not only my son but *all* creation.

It was not that I expected some sort of miraculous or sudden return to sanity and health for my son, nor that it would come to pass if only I prayed and believed hard enough. This invitation was to a faith more raw and naked than I had previously known. Rather than miracles in the sense of a sudden return to sanity, this faith meant an utter reliance on powers not my own, even as I did what was in my power to protect my son and to get help for him. It required a deeper confidence that we would be held and upheld through all the unknowns and uncertainty that surrounded us as well as lay ahead of us. It meant a trust beyond words. It meant that "You've got to believe."

Seven or eight years before that trip to Nicaragua I had been teaching a confirmation class for ninth graders. With ninth graders, you never really know if being in a confirmation class is their idea or their parents', but it's a safe assumption that it's probably the latter. Toward the end of their year of study I asked each of the students to write a "faith statement," which I explained by saying, "Tell me what your faith is at this point, what you affirm, what you have doubts about, what speaks to you, and what you struggle with."

One young man in the class seemed an excellent candidate for "Least Likely to Complete the Assignment." He was a bright kid but did not seem much engaged with the prospect of confirmation. His body language and demeanor said, "This is my parents' idea. Can I leave now?" Imagine my surprise when his faith statement began with a sentence that sent a chill up my spine. "I believe in believing," he wrote simply. He played an electric guitar and this sentence sounded like a song lyric, and maybe it is. Such a sentiment or conviction can, of course, be seen as saying far too little, even as glib. But it didn't strike me that way. It struck me as something bold and good, a declaration of one's colors in the face of ironic sophistication and widespread cynicism of contemporary American culture. There was a time when faith was the easy option and reflected a consensus in Western society, but that's no longer the case. Believing in God, in something holy, in grace, in a power—as Montaigne once wrote, "That is always on the side of those brave enough to trust it"—is no longer the safe choice, it is the risky choice.

When my son and I returned to Seattle from Nicaragua, and not without a lot of help, the snow was gone, but a long winter was just beginning for our family. We lived through, and worked through, a great deal of loss, bewilderment, and pain over the next two years as God held both us and our son. It seemed, no matter how sick he became, that there was also something in him that sought health. It was that something that led him to get on the plane back to Managua from Nicaragua's east coast, and in time to return home. My wife and I walked the line that caring parents must walk, between holding on and letting go. But the words that stayed with me and held me through the long journey toward his recovery were those he had spoken beneath the trees: "You've got to believe."

# FAITH AND ITS
# DISTORTIONS

WHAT WE WANT to know," began the spokesman for a group of ten people who confronted me on a warm August day. "What we want to know," he repeated as if to add both gravity and emphasis, "is, have you been born again?" It was not a straightforward question or simple inquiry. It was a loaded question, a test question. I was being tested. I was on the spot.

I was twenty-eight years old at the time, and had been serving my first congregation for only a month or so, since graduating from seminary. It turned out I walked into the middle of a war zone. The congregation was divided into what felt like armed camps. The "presenting issue," as therapists like to say, was a position taken by our denomination in support of civil rights for persons who are gay and lesbian. For the group of church members who now confronted me, it was an appalling thing to advocate and a clear abandonment of faith's essentials. The other camp in the congregation took the opposite stand. Those members not in either camp, which was most of the congregation, were unsure what they thought or where they stood on this issue, and some hadn't even decided if they really cared what the denomination had done.

The people who confronted me that day were the loudest and most sure of themselves of the combatants in the congregational war zone. They had been "born again." They were right, or at least they thought so. Having now listened to a couple of my sermons they decided it was time to get things, meaning me, pinned down. Which side was I on? Whose side was I on? "What we want to know is, have you been born again?"

At that moment, I was pretty shaky inside. Very little in my background or my years at a liberal seminary in New York had prepared me for this. My life did not flash before my eyes as they waited on my answer, but certain questions definitely did. Questions like, "What in the world am I doing here?" and "Why did I think this was a good idea?" Outwardly I smiled, trying my best to relieve some of the tension in the air as well as in my churning innards. The faces of my interrogators were tight, flushed, and intense. "Well," I said, with a smile that belied my inner panic, "I guess the proof is in the pudding." Then, thinking that it might help my cause to invoke Scripture, I hastily added, "Or as our Lord said, 'By their fruits ye shall know them.'" "But answer our question," demanded one large man, his face flushed red. "Now, Fred," said his wife. "C'mon now," he said, "'By their fruits ye shall know them.' That's right, c'mon." Whether with the smile or the Scripture, or the combination of the two, I had won the skirmish. They retreated, but they would be back.

I learned something as I looked into their eyes that day. There was not going to be any reasoning with, or even really conversing with, most of these folks. Their eyes were fixed and hard. They looked at you but didn't see you. They looked right through you. Part of it, of course, is that they were angry. Anger tends to narrow your perceptual field quite considerably. But it was more than that. They had the truth, and they were out to see if you, actually me, fit it. If not, you were an enemy. If you weren't "us," you were "them." You were expendable. I learned this lesson that day: There is a difference between ideology and faith.

Ideology means that you have the Truth. You possess it like a dog possesses a bone, and you are prepared to defend it aggressively if need be. Ambiguity, which biologist and essayist Lewis Thomas somewhere described as "The sure knowledge that the ground beneath your feet is always shifting," and the condition of being human, has been overcome and eliminated with ideology. To Thomas's way of thinking, the ability to tolerate ambiguity is central to being human. My party of ten would not have agreed. With the grasping of Truth and possession of it whole and unimpaired, there is no discussion, not really; nor is debate necessary. Even the simple give and take of conversation is hardly permitted. Ideology sooner or later reveals itself clearly in its resort to coercive power. The bone is picked up and turned into a club. Those who don't go along are pressured into silence or bludgeoned into submission.

It seems that many people today, both those who consider themselves religious and those who are quite sure they're not and want nothing to do with religion, confuse ideology and faith. Ideology is knowing that you know, and possessing certainty. Faith, while not without core convictions and assurances, is at least in part knowing that you don't know. Not fully, not completely. Faith is knowing that we don't know fully, completely, or finally, and yet trusting, as the apostle Paul said, that we are fully known.

To trust in God, a higher power, or powers of blessing not your own is to know that you are not God. It is to know that neither you, nor your tribe or nation, nor your church or movement have the complete or the absolute or total truth. Because

God is God, and not you, you remain limited in your knowledge, in your power, and in your sight and insight. That is to
say, you remain human, which is not a bad thing to be, but it is
sometimes a hard thing to be. We would prefer living without
such limitations.

There is a wonderful little Islamic story according to
which the prophet Mohammed revealed ninety-nine of the
one hundred names of God to his followers. But Mohammed
whispered the one-hundredth name of God only to his camel.
Why? Why tell the secret to a camel? Because, no one should
know everything there is to know about God. Moreover, no
one does. The camel didn't spill the beans.

Being human, insofar as it means being limited and therefore vulnerable, is not easy. But claiming to be more than
human, and to possess God-like knowledge and truth, very
quickly becomes demonic and dangerous, especially when you
are part of a religion that is really an ideology that serves to
sanction and bless political movements or national causes. Then
it is a real problem in the making.

It should be said here that neither side of the political or
religious or social spectrum has a monopoly on the ideology
thing. Currently, the right wing in American politics and
religion seems more organized and to some more ominously
ideological, but people on the left are equally capable of ideological fixations and justifications. Even those who claim to be
open-minded can be so committed to their open-mindedness
that nothing else seems to be permitted to challenge their self-
understanding. The novelist Flannery O'Connor captured this
quality, in a characteristically tart phrase, when she spoke of
"the invincibly ignorant."[1]

Moreover, the recourse to ideology is hardly beyond our
understanding. Quite the contrary, it is entirely understandable.

Ideology deals handily with the primal human problems of uncertainty, vulnerability, and the continuous ambiguity of life. It delivers us from them, albeit at a terrible price. Moreover, ideology is a response to the more recent problem of information overload. Ideology becomes a way of sorting through and leaving out. I listen to this, not that; I talk to them, but not to others, because this fits with the way I have the world already set and ordered. Here we are all, in some measure, implicated.

When the Protestant reformer John Calvin was converted, he described his conversion in a way that would, I suspect, surprise many today. By his conversion Calvin received, he said, "A teachable spirit . . . God by a sudden conversion subdued and brought my mind to a teachable frame which was more hardened in such matters than might have been expected from one at my early period of life."[2] Conversion did not mean, as so many seem to think of it today, gaining possession of the total and complete truth or having all the answers. Rather, Calvin's conversion meant knowing that he did not know, and receiving a pliability of spirit—a vulnerability—in place of his hardened heart. Soft flesh for hard metal; it was a good trade. Conversion was not, as it so often seems today, an ending and a finished point. It was a beginning and an opening point. Experientially, it is closer to waking up after a long sleep.

While writing an essay on "Why I Became a Minister" and finding myself stalled, I decided to try a writer's exercise about which I had recently read. Called "Random Words," it consists of opening a dictionary at any page and plunking down your finger on a random word. Then you look for connections. Are there connections between what you're trying to write about and the word you have fingered? I suppose it is often a stretch, but that's the point, to stretch your thinking, to loosen your mind and stir your imagination.

The word I fingered that day was *placoid*, which means "plate-like, as in the hard, tooth-like scales of shark, skate, or ray." *Placoid* and "Why I Became a Minister"? Hmmm. Actually it did connect, almost too easily. I was a pretty taut young man as I left home to go to college. In college and subsequently in graduate school I learned that I could harden my shell against the world by putting on intellectual armor. With wit and intelligence I could not only protect myself but even wound others and keep them at a safe distance. When the road forked with academia down one path and ministry down the other, I chose the latter. At least in part, I chose it as a way of shedding my placoid skin. Like a snake, I crawled out of it, leaving it behind as evidence of my moving on.

So Calvin's conversion story makes sense to me. Conversion is not shutting down, but opening up. Not case closed, but mystery open. It's no longer pretending that you know, but cheerfully accepting that you don't know, or at least don't know it all. And faith is living in a relationship with a truth and love one can never fully possess or fathom, exhaust or capture.

I realize that some of what we know as Christianity, and much of what many have experienced as Christianity, is much more nearly like what I am calling "ideology" than what I am calling "faith." That is a perennial danger in all religions. Moreover, there are reasons for that in Christianity's case. Some are historical and cultural. In the fourth century, Christianity became the official religion of the waning Roman Empire, and subsequently of the West. Any religion that gets wrapped up in official garb is likely to get turned into a religion that claims to have all the truth and all the answers. There are also human reasons for it. Being human, which means being limited and vulnerable, ain't easy. It can be positively frightening at times, and it would appear to be so for many in our own times. Such fear should not be dismissed or discounted. But sometimes we humans will do most anything to overcome our fearfulness and anxiety, including saying "yes" when what we should be saying is "no," or "I don't know," or "Let me get back to you on that."

On that warm and sunny August day, standing outside my first church, ten angry people before me, I was struck by the irony that what Jesus meant by "born again" is just about 180 degrees in the opposite direction from how it was understood by my interrogators. As novelist Walker Percy's character Will Barrett says in *The Second Coming*, "If the born again are the twice born, I'm holding out for the third go-around."[3]

In the biblical story that includes the phrase "born again," Jesus tells a religious leader and official, Nicodemus (who thought he knew exactly what was what, thanks very much), that being born again is all about starting over completely, becoming like a little child, knowing that you don't know everything, and that it is exactly what Nicodemus needs. Alas, Nicodemus didn't get it. In one of the great literalist failures in recorded Scripture he asks Jesus, "Can one enter a second time into the mother's womb and be born?" (John 3:4). It is comforting to know that Jesus' preachments didn't always get through either.

Sometime not long after the Berlin wall fell, a thirteen-year-old girl from formerly communist Berlin made her way to some sort of Christian community in the western part of the city and took shelter there. Several years before the wall fell she had been sold into prostitution by her mother. She had known little in her short life save peril, fear, and abuse. Day by day she seemed to gain something in strength living in the shelter of the community. One day, there was the celebration of a baptism. The minister or priest who presided spoke of being born again, born anew from above, and of baptism as a new birth.

The girl had no background in a faith or a church and had never heard of baptism before. She had never before heard the words "born again." The phrase had not been turned into a slogan or code. Thanks to communism and her upbringing, she was on these matters *tabula rasa*. The language was all new and fresh for her. After the baptism she made her way toward the fount, where the water gleamed as sunlight played upon it. In a literal and completely naïve way, the child, tears in her eyes, asked the minister, "Can I be born again? Can I start new, start fresh? Can I start over?" Her questions had none of the ideological charge of those who asked their test question of me. But she was ever so much closer, or so I think, to the heart of the matter.

# ON GRACE

*THIS IS a letter that I wrote several years ago to
my daughter, Laura, about what I believe is the heart
of Christian faith, the concept and experience of grace.
She was fourteen when I wrote this letter to her.*

**D**EAR LAURA, WHEN your mother and I were falling in love we happened to spend a day together on
the Oregon coast. As we walked along the beach I
carved five letters, each about twelve feet high, into the sand.
When I was done it spelled LUCKY, and that's how I felt. Incredibly lucky to be in love, to be loved by the woman who was
to become your mother. It was all a gift, and I knew it. I didn't
deserve this wondrous thing that had happened to me, nor had
I managed to bring it about by my ardent and clever courting.
It was grace.

Grace means something like this: You are loved not because
you are always lovable or deserving or appealing or because
you have measured up to some standard, but just because. Just
because that's the way God is. God loves freely, even recklessly.

Before our faith in God is God's faith in us. God's faith in us is grace. God's actions on our behalf are grace.

For me grace has been a genuine lifesaver. Through some combination of circumstances I got the notion as I grew up that if only I tried hard enough and was good enough, I would then be loved, by God, by my parents, by the world, and by myself. The catch was that I had to be on my toes at all times, and striving always for achievement, distinction, and perfection. I had to shine brighter and do better than others. There are at least two problems with this. The first is that it is a terrible lot of work. The second is that it doesn't work.

Striving to achieve, to stand out, to be better and smarter than the next person is not only an awful lot of work, it's not particularly happy or enjoyable work. You can pretty easily end up like the elder brother in Jesus' parable of the Prodigal Son (Luke 15:11-32). When the father in that story forgave his younger and prodigal son and even made a fool of himself by running out to meet his errant and lost, but now returning boy, the elder brother was completely beside himself. He couldn't stand it. He was fuming.

His father's forgiving and joyous welcome of his ne'er-do-well brother drove the elder brother berserk. It was not fair. The elder brother had worked himself to a frazzle, day after livelong day. He had been the good son who had kept the family farm going, without any help from his no-good brother, thanks very much. Now, after that same brother had squandered a sizeable chunk of the family fortune, their father does not demand that junior shape up, or that he work off the debt. Instead, the old man goes running down the road, making an utter fool of himself, falling all over the boy, and then he throws a party for him. When the elder brother comes in from his day's labors in the fields, hot and sweaty, he can't believe it.

The sound of the party in progress is like a slap in the face. He is furious. He kept the rules and where did it get him? In so many words he complains to his father, "You've never thrown a party like this for me!!"

The elder brother fumed because it was not fair. And he was right. Grace is not fair. When we believe that everyone should get just what they deserve, no more and no less, and that life should operate on a strict system of fairness and just deserts, grace and forgiveness and mercy *are* offensive. Grace means that when we deserve a closed door, we find an open one instead. Grace means that when we ought to be tossed in the penalty box, we get a party. Grace means that when we deserve a slap in the face, we get smothered in an embrace.

The problem confronting the elder brother in the parable, a problem I've struggled with throughout my life (I am also an elder brother), is really a human problem. It is my observation that most of us think that we play by the rules, and that we darn well deserve what we get in the way of life's benefits and blessings. Many of us, in fact, are forever nursing a sense of grievance and resentment because we feel we deserve better than we've received. We can't stand it when someone who doesn't play by the rules, at least as we see it and according to our scorekeeping, is rewarded. And of course in the normal day-to-day living of life, fairness is important. Important, but not enough.

From God's point of view, perhaps none of us plays perfectly and wholly by the rules. Maybe from God's point of view all of us look a whole lot more like prodigal younger sons, even us hardworking, older brothers and sisters. You see, the elder son is in his own particular way as distant from his father as his brother has been. True, he never left home. But plodding along day after day, imagining that he could gain his father's love and the family estate by his hard work, he missed a crucial fact: his father loved him all along and everything that the father had was already his. Unfortunately, however, the elder brother had never found any joy in that love or in his work. He missed the grace every bit as much as his younger brother had. Like the father in the story, God loves us all, elder brothers (and sisters) too. Not because we have earned it, but because that's the way God is.

Here's what it comes down to: Christianity is a religion of grace. It is not a religion of virtue, nor a religion of rules. What's the difference? A religion of virtue or of rules says that "If you measure up, if you are good enough, if you are truly virtuous, then God will love you." A religion of grace says, "God loves you—that's the given. Because God loves you, act as if you are beloved." Grace comes first.

That, by the way, is how it is throughout the Bible, in story after story. The grace and gift of freedom comes first in the story of Exodus. Only afterward are the Hebrew people led to Mount Sinai and given the Ten Commandments (the Law). In the Bible, the law is how people who are loved and know it, how people who have experienced grace and mercy, are to shape their lives and their life together. Grace comes first.

It's the same in the New Testament. The grace of the resurrection comes first, which brings with it a second chance for the disciples of Jesus who had deserted and denied him when the chips were down. Only after the disciples are astonished that God has not deserted and forsaken them, but come to them once again, and that Jesus is in some strange way alive, only then is the church called into being. Grace comes first.

That is the grammar of the Gospel, or "good news." Grace and response. First comes grace, then our response. Whenever and wherever Christians and the church have forgotten this,

Christianity has turned into something that is moralistic and legalistic and joyless. It turns into a religion that is all about keeping the rules, or pretending to, about appearances, about our deciding who's in and who's out. It turns, in other words, into a religion that is all about us and our doing, and not a bit about God and God's amazing grace. It turns into a religion of good works and achievement and ceases to be a religion of grace. When this happens it is only a matter of time until God breaks in to blow the whole thing sky high.

Not too many years ago there was an evangelistic campaign that tried to win people to Christianity. The slogan of the campaign was "I found it!" I guess that meant, I found the truth, or I found God, or I found love. I always thought they had it backwards. I thought the slogan should have been "It found me!" At least that's the way I've experienced it. Or as John Newton put it in his famous hymn "Amazing Grace," "I once was lost but now am found, was blind but now I see."

*Love, Dad*

# THE OTHER SIDE
# OF GRACE

GRACE IS NOT only the prodigal's unexpected (and undeserved) party. Nor is grace only amazing forgiveness and redemption. Grace has another side, as Flannery O'Connor explored in her fiction, a darker and more violent side. For the self-righteous and self-absorbed, grace has a hard side, which is important. Without this, grace risks going saccharine, a sweetness that is of no nutritional value and which may even be cancer causing.

This is a story of the other side, the harder side, of grace. After not quite four years as pastor at my first church we pulled up stakes, moving from that small town in the foothills of the Cascade Mountains in Washington State to Honolulu, Hawaii, where I had accepted a new pastoral position. I had been called to Church of the Crossroads. Was it an authentic call of God or the siren song of personal ambition? Can the two, as I suspect, be all wrapped up together? It is never easy to know. What was clear is that we left a lot behind. If you're lucky, a first church for a new pastor is like a first love, sweet and incomparable. Our second child had been born during that first ministry. The church had gone from conflict and disarray to promise and vitality, a transformation symbolized by the planning and completion of a building program. Both our family and the church had been deeply involved in welcoming nearly seventy Hmong refugees, casualties of the Vietnam War, to that small, agricultural community along the Snoqualmie River. We were loved, and we loved back. We left it all behind and went west, further west, to the middle of the Pacific Ocean.

I like a challenge and my new church in Hawaii certainly presented one. As late as the mid-1960s it had been a congregation of eight hundred members. Now, in the early 1980s, the membership stood below two hundred. What happened? Lots of things. The Vietnam era, during which the church gave sanctuary to soldiers who refused to return to combat from furlough; the pastor's embrace of the "death of God" theology of the late sixties; the general crisis of confidence in institutions and authority of the late sixties and seventies; the gradual development of a homeless population living on the open grounds of the church campus. Many of the nearly two hundred members who were still part of the congregation by the time I arrived weren't on particularly good terms with one another; conflicts and disagreements had been simply piled, one on top of another, rather than processed or resolved. Some thought the homeless people living on the grounds of the church were a kind of reincarnation of Jack Kerouac or the true spirit of the sixties, while others viewed them as bums and thugs (neither was right). My predecessor had ended her pastorate by taking her own life, a sad bit of information I did not learn until I had arrived.

I arrived with an agenda. Of course it included getting the lay of the land and the sense of the spiritual and emotional condition of the congregation. But I was determined to "turn the church around." I had been seduced by those who said I was just the right person to do that, to restore the church to its former strength and glory. I believed them. I had been seduced by my own vanity. Not only did I have my "turn it around" agenda, I had another kind of agenda of which I myself was only partially aware. I was becoming an odd new creature, what someone would soon dub a "theological post-liberal." I had been formed by theological liberalism, but was also critical of it. Moreover, I was beginning to see, or maybe "feel" would be closer to the mark, that a certain era in the life of the Protestant churches in America was ending. It was not long before the widespread institutional decline of such churches and denominations confirmed my sense of an ending, but in 1981 and at age thirty-two I only sensed what I could not yet name. A world was dying, the world of American Christendom and civic faith, the world in which the Protestant mainline churches were the religious establishment of American culture and society. What was to come was hidden in the future.

During that first year in Hawaii I worked my tail off. Mostly what I got for my labors was resistance. Probably that's an overstatement or even misstatement. I got a lot of support, but one indicator flashing red for many leaders is that they see and hear the negatives so much more powerfully than the positives. And I did. I was hurt by the negative comments and those who manipulated things to protect their turf and interests. Only much later would I understand the wisdom of the teacher of leadership, Ron Heifetz, who wrote, "You appear dangerous to people when you question their values, beliefs, or habits of a lifetime. You place yourself on the line when you tell people what they need to hear rather than what they want to hear."[4] Young and foolish, I expected people to thank me, even love me, for telling them what they did not wish to hear. Only later did I hear and understand the ironic wisdom of "No good deed goes unpunished."

Returning from vacation and beginning my second year at my new church, I hit a wall. It was bad, and I had no idea what "it" was or what in the world was going on. What I did know was that my energy, my élan vital, had drained away. I spent long stretches staring at the wall and the ceiling. I felt like there was a hollow place—a painful, hollow place—where my chest had been. I was lost, adrift, clueless, and astonished.

I began what proved to be a long journey through a long line of "helping professionals." First, I went to see a fellow pastor. After a time, he suggested I visit with a hospital chaplain of his acquaintance. After several sessions with the chaplain, he sent me on to a psychotherapist. Then to a psychiatrist. Then to another psychiatrist. Each new step seemed to take me deeper into some world I never imagined would be mine. Of course, this all took time and money. Moreover, it was strange. I wasn't used to seeking or needing help. I was supposed to give help. The diagnosis was depression, a malady to which ministers, I have subsequently learned, seem particularly prone. I was at the five-year mark as a pastor, an exit point for many in the ordained ministry who conclude that God has something else in mind for them besides being a pastor. The truth is, it's a tough way to make a living.

"Have you considered other kinds of work?" asked the psychiatrist. "Maybe you're not cut out to be a minister." Then he wrote a prescription for an antidepressant drug, hopefully named, Ascenden. This was before the newer and more effective depression drugs of the late eighties. Ascenden didn't do much for me, so far as I could tell. I continued to live in a kind of fog. And I continued, doggedly, stubbornly, to be a pastor.

But I did some other things too. I found my way to a place called The Spiritual Life Center. It was a converted convent, now a retreat center. A couple of older Maryknoll sisters ran the place. I took the elevator up to the third floor, and lugged my bag to my spartan room. Then I went to see my "spiritual director," Sr. Katherine, who looked like my Aunt Vera, plump and friendly. She chuckled like my Aunt Vera. She didn't cook like my Aunt Vera, which was just as well because I was one of those inclined to try to eat my way out of my depression. Sr. Katherine offered nutrition of a different sort: Scripture, meditation, prayer, and rest. She gave me my first biblical passage, from Isaiah 43, and sent me off to "pray the Scriptures," a new idea and experience for me. I was used to analyzing the Scriptures, but not to praying them. She said, "Pray it over several times. See what words or phrases touch you or speak to you. Go with those. Let them take you where they will." And as I headed off she added, smiling, "And if you should get sleepy, take a nap. It's OK. You're probably exhausted. Most pastors are."

That was the first of several three-day silent retreats over the next several years. But they weren't silent, not really. It was only that no person was speaking. In that silence, the Holy Spirit had a chance. That first passage was like medicine for the soul, no, *it was medicine for my soul.* "When you pass through the waters, I will be with you; and through the rivers, they shall not overwhelm you; when you walk through fire you shall not be burned, and the flame shall not consume you" (Isa. 43:2). "Do not fear, for I have redeemed you; I have called you by name, you are mine" (Isa. 43:1). For the first time in a long time it felt as if I could breathe again.

The next day the Scripture to be prayed was from the Gospel of John, chapter 15, verses 1-8. After Isaiah's words of affirmation and encouragement, came a reminder, one that had an edge to it. "I am the vine, you are the branches" (v. 5). "He removes every branch in me that bears no fruit. Every branch that bears fruit he prunes to make it bear more fruit" (v. 2). Am

I a branch being removed, for that is surely what it felt like, or am I being pruned? How do you know the difference between pruning and being removed?

More important was verse 5, the verse that restores the proper relationship: "I am the vine, you are the branches. Those who abide in me, and I in them bear much fruit." Slowly I realized and admitted that I was mostly trying to do this thing by myself. I was trying to play all the roles: vine, branches, and vinedresser. I was trying to be God, to do it all, and to do it all with my own strength alone. The word was simple, elegant, and painful: "It's not about you. Oh, to be sure, you are wonderful and I do love you, and you have your part to play and your work to do. But, really, it's not about you. Do you think you could let God be God for you?" Like so many of us in ministry, I preached grace, but didn't believe it was for me, not really. I had to earn it. The truth is that this is a clever way of keeping yourself in control, or at least maintaining the illusion that you are in control. So, depressed at the lack of results from our relentless and virtuous labors, we labor harder and longer. And what do you get for working more? You get more work. A strange thing, and some of us figure that out very, very slowly.

Bottom line: Depression has a hard core of self-centeredness. That may be difficult for many of us to imagine, much less swallow, because a big part of it is feeling pretty awful about who you are or who you *think* you are. But the point remains: It is you that you are fixed upon, centered upon, fixated over. Get over it. Let God be God. Let God be God for you.

Slowly, the wall I'd hit revealed a door, a door that had been open all along, and which opened from the other side. Slowly, I began to learn not a whole new way of living, but steps, small steps on a path. One of the big small steps is perspective. Perspective on oneself and on the particular challenges you have chosen to work on. Mine included a congregation that had been through years of very tough stuff. They needed change and direction. They also needed love and patience. Perspective dawned as well, albeit more slowly, about the great shift in the religious ecology, the sea change, that was so large as to be nearly imperceptible. An era, American Christendom and modernity, was ending. It was big, I realized. I would be about the work of this dying and some new rising for my entire career as a minister. We wouldn't fix this by Tuesday. It would be a life journey and a life's work, not an item on a check-off list. Several years later I would come upon a line from an Old Testament scholar that caught the largeness of it. "The world for which you have been so carefully preparing is being taken away from you, by the grace of God."

Was I cured? Not completely, not wholly. Like the biblical Jacob, I walk with a limp, evidence of the struggle. Not a literal limp, but a reminder of my tendency to get confused about who's God. "There is a God, John," says the note on the refrigerator of a friend, "and it's not you." Like Jacob, I have been wounded but blessed. Out of the struggle has emerged a strange and wondrous blessing. Not only do I understand myself a little better, and take myself a little less seriously, I have some sort of understanding, from the inside, of the struggle of religious as well as other sorts of leaders. I have been able to take my own experience and derive some value and meaning for the larger context of the huge challenges facing the church in a new time. It works just so long as I remember "I am the vine, you are the branches."

# REVELATION

GIVING UP, RELINQUISHING his search for the burning bush, and tired from a day of rambling, Lane turned back towards his cabin. On the way he caught sight of a small clearing that seemed somehow, though for no apparent reason, to beckon to him. It was covered with leaves, dimly lit, and yet somehow inviting. He entered the clearing, and weary from his day-long search for wonder, rested on a fallen tree. How long he waited there, he could not say. Suddenly a sound rustled amid the trees and brush just beyond the clearing and to his right. The sound was, however, different from that made by the chipmunks and small birds. It was heavier, made by something large. He waited, still and silent, feeling not only the weight of it but also its consciousness. Then he saw it. It was a deer, a young doe. While he remained still, the deer gradually made its way into the clearing when suddenly she saw him. She stopped fast, stamping her right front hoof, moving her head up and down, then side to side, and finally wagging her tail fiercely. Her liquid eyes seemed to look through the man. For a moment she jumped back into the brush, but he waited, unmoving, and she returned. After a few more minutes, she continued in the direction she had been heading and disappeared.

Theologian Belden Lane, in his book *Landscapes of the Sacred*, tells a simple story, one that makes me nod in recognition. Worn out by daily life, the combination of routine and responsibility, and saying "yes" to far too many things, he went off by himself to the wooded land and cliffs north of St. Louis where the Illinois and Missouri Rivers have their confluence. He went in search of mystery, of holiness, and with a fevered longing for some grand and mystic encounter. He searched all day long. "But God," he reported, "would not be caught. I would drag the bag and snare back empty, no trophies to mount."[5]

That was it, not much by some notions of revelation, and yet quite enough by others. "The uncanny thing," remarked Lane, "was that I had been invited to the place. I had *felt* the deer (I felt some presence) in the clearing a good ten or fifteen minutes *before* she came."[6] It was a gift. Moreover, the story points to an axiom regarding sacred places: "Sacred place is not chosen, it chooses." It has about it the dynamics of revelation, of the intrusion upon us of another reality, another power.

His fevered search for wonder or holiness yielded no result. Just when he had given up, it found him, it came to him. This is the nature of revelation and of revelatory experience. We do not so much choose it as it chooses us. We experience a sense of a presence, of encounter or being encountered. Such experience or awareness of revelation is at the root of religious experience and sensitivity.

That said, *revelation* seems to be a lost word among us, surrendered to television evangelists or attached to the forbidding final book of the Bible, and the even more forbidding interpretations of it. *Revelation* means that something hidden is revealed, something covered or obscured is made manifest and visible. It has the quality of coming to us, even at us, rather than from us. It is not something we choose. It chooses.

In precisely this way such experiences provide an antidote and alternative to what seems the predominant way of life. These days life often seems something we can only imagine ourselves being in charge of. There is a good deal of talk today about our many choices and how it is up to us to choose our own lives. Of course, there is some bit of truth in this kind of talk, but less I think than we imagine. It rests on an illusion, namely, that we are in control. In so many ways our lives seem to choose us. We might be closer to an honest and more truthful understanding of life were we to recognize the illusion behind our modern notion that we *are* in control, or even worse, that we *should* be in control of life.

The alternative to our devotion to control and choosing is not, however, being passive before life. It is to understand life, as our forebears by and large did, as that which addresses us and to which we may, and even must, respond. "Religion begins," observed Rabbi Abraham Heschel, "with an awareness that something is being asked of us." We human beings are answerers. In this way of construing life, we are being addressed and spoken to continuously by life and being itself, though in a thousand small increments. Life is revealing itself to us. It is our calling as human beings to answer life's challenge and mystery—its revelations, if you will—by our lives, and to do so with as much courage and wit as possible.

Another, older way of putting this is to speak of "rising to the occasion." I recall a newly widowed elderly woman, who was asked about the death of her beloved husband. "What was she going do about it?" said someone, foolishly I thought. "Do about it?" she repeated. "Well, there's nothing to do about it, only to rise to the occasion as best I can." She understood that we do not control life. Life and being address us, and we have, or hope to have, the wherewithal to answer. For the most part, we can't control what life brings us. It is, however, up to us how we respond to life. Something is being asked of us.

# DREAMS

WHAT I MOST love about dreams is that they are given. They are not something we get, but something we are given. So far as I know, you can't make dreams happen, nor should we want to. Perhaps you can invite dreams, even in some ways cultivate them, but they remain gifts. They have the quality of a visitation. Someone, something arrives unbidden and unexpected. Of course, dreams do not always feel as if they are a good gift or a friendly visitor. We have bad dreams. But even they are given, not something we get.

One category of my dreams is dreams about one of my three children. Parents dream of their children. Sometimes such dreams are anxiety laden, for what is a parent's lot if not to worry? But often these dreams of my children contain a blessing. My own most telling and prophetic dream came to me in the summer before our eldest set out to go to college. I had an elaborate dream in which he was in considerable peril. At a particular point in the dream he was being lowered by ropes into some deep and hidden mountain crevasse, where he disappeared from view. We could no longer see him. He was hidden from us.

What was required of my wife and I, his parents, in the dream was to let him go. We had to drop the ropes that held him, and release him. We were to trust that he would emerge

again on some other side, alive and whole. Insofar as its prophecy, this dream turned out to have little to do with his actual
college years. College would seem tame and safe by comparison to what followed. It was after his graduation that he did
seem to disappear, to be hidden from us and lost to us. The year
after graduation, he went into the deep and hidden crevasse of
bipolar illness.

As his parents we learned, slowly and painfully, an important distinction, one that had a great deal to do with the dream's
business of binding and holding. In one very real sense, we
could and must hold him. We could and we did support him
during those dark years. And yet, it was also true, and in a way
more true, that we could not hold onto him. We had to let
him go and trust him to God as well as his own better angels,
even as we provided, in and through our home and family and
love, a holding vessel. Somehow I imagine this is the way God
loves each of us. Not by holding onto us, preventing us from
all harm or every danger, but by holding us *in the midst of* harm
and danger.

This distinction was brought home to me early on in the
most traumatic period of his illness. Recently home from his
first and only hospitalization, and still quite agitated, he charged
into the kitchen one evening as I was washing dishes. He
clutched an amber-tinted bottle of pills. Thrusting it towards
me he said, with considerable energy and defiance, "You can't
make me take these!" Whether by the grace of God or some
other wisdom, I said nothing at all for perhaps a minute. I continued washing dishes. He stood waiting. Then I turned to him
and said, "You're right. You'll have to decide to do that yourself." We could and would hold him, providing a home and
family that loved him through this dark time. But we could
not hold onto him. I could not make him take the prescribed

medication. "You'll have to decide to do that yourself." The energy of that confrontation subsided. He left me to the dishes. He decided to take the medicine. We hold, but we do not hold onto, that is, control others, even or perhaps especially our own children.

This distinction by which we hold and let go also validated the different perspectives of my wife and I as we struggled before his diagnosis and during his treatment. My wife leaned toward holding on, and did so, at times desperately. I leaned toward letting go, and at times did so, with impatience and wariness. Pressing our own perspectives and their duality, we never imagined that we were both right. The situation required holding him *and* letting go of him. The dream stayed with me throughout those difficult times, sometimes a comfort, sometimes a challenge. In time and by the grace of God, our son did emerge from the crevasse to another side of health and a greater wholeness.

Now that I am older, I also dream of my own parents. Recently I dreamt of my father, who died several years ago. As a pastor, I have often listened to people speak of dreaming of loved ones who have died. Mostly these dreams seem reassuring to people, and my dream of my father was like that. I can't remember that anything particular happened. He was there, I was there. He was himself. He was at peace. We were easy together, which was not always the case when he was alive. I awoke feeling distinctly comforted and blessed. He and I could go on, separate and yet always together, which is I suppose the place parents and children long to be and need to be: apart and together, distinct and yet in strange and irrevocable communion, at one and the same time.

Under the influence of modernity with its overdose of reason and rationality, Western spirituality and religion have not made too much of dreams. But dreams and visions are plentiful in the Bible. The two great biblical dreamers are both named Joseph, which happens to be the name of our eldest son, who was the subject of my crevasse dream. The first biblical Joseph is the boy with the coat of many colors. His life alternates between the pit and the palace. He starts in the palace of his father, Jacob's, special love. Joseph is the only son of Jacob's beloved wife Rachel and for that reason is special to his father. But before long, Joseph is cast down into a pit by the jealousy and hatred of his eleven half-brothers. Their hostility is not without basis because Joseph has the annoying habit of reminding his brothers that he was the special and most beloved son.

Rescued from that particular pit, he rose to prominence in Egypt, only to be cast down again, to a prison on the trumped-up rape charges of a spurned woman, Potiphar's wife. But it is Joseph's capacity to make sense of dreams, his own and those of others, that proves his ticket out of Pharoah's dungeon and back into the palace. Famously, Joseph's dream of seven starving cattle predicts the seven lean years of famine ahead. Thus warned, Egypt prepares for the lean years by stockpiling grain. This weaves back into the larger story of God's plan and purpose when Joseph's brothers arrive, hats in hands, in Pharoah's court seeking grain for their starving family. Joseph, it turns out, has been placed in Egypt to ensure that this odd family, which God in his inscrutable wisdom had chosen to be blessed and to be a blessing, would survive.

Dreams are also survival tools for the second biblical Joseph, husband of Mary, who dreams at all the crucial moments in order to receive direction. His first important dream comes at the point when he discovers that his bride-to-be is with child and he knows only one thing for sure: The child Mary carries is not his. Joseph's first dream overrules both law and propriety and leads him to risk all by keeping on with Mary and marrying her, thus taking the infant Jesus as his own son. After the birth of Jesus, Joseph's second dream warns him to flee Herod's pogrom against all newborn Hebrew boys. And, in a nice touch, it is to Egypt that the holy family takes flight and in which they find refuge until Herod dies and they can safely return to Israel.

Dreams are not, at least in the biblical stories, ends in themselves. Nor are they magic to be manipulated or used to further personal ambitions. They are in service of some larger plan, the unfolding of the often hidden and mysterious plan and purpose of God. Dreams and their cousin, visions, are both a sign and means by which God works out God's purposes, by which God works redemption. Perhaps God resorts to dreams and often appears to people in the night because only then are our defenses lowered or relaxed enough that God has a chance of getting through to us.

# GOSPEL: PROBLEM
# AND PARADOX

CHRISTIANITY IS SO regularly presented as the solution to our problems that it does not usually occur to us that it is also and more often the *problem* for our solutions. That is, the Gospel raises questions about the ways we have things put together, the ways that we have explained ourselves and others and the world to ourselves. But it is just then, when our tried-and-true explanations break down, when our confident ways of seeing are shown to be but forms of blindness, that something interesting, something transformative might happen.

Many, if not most, of Jesus' parables operate this way—that is, they challenge conventional wisdom and turn things upside down. They provoke a breakdown that can become a breakthrough. Consider Jesus' strange parable of the vineyard workers in Matthew, chapter 20. Jesus tells the story of the vineyard owner, who at harvest time goes into the market to hire workers. He goes early in the morning to hire a first group, for which they negotiate to receive the the customary daily wage. As the day goes on the vineyard owner returns to the market square four times; each time he hires more workers. Finally, with only one hour left in the work day, he hires another and last group.

At quitting time the workers line up to be paid, beginning at the head of the line with those last to arrive. Surprise, they are paid the whole day's wage for one hour of work, as were the workers in the next group who had worked only three hours. The half-day and all-day workers farther back in the line see what is going on and assume that they will be paid more than they had been originally promised since they had worked the entire day. But they don't receive more. They are paid exactly the same as the others, exactly what they bargained for, and they are not happy.

Once while I was leading a group study of this parable, after we finished reading it over a couple of times, one person blurted out, "I am not sure I know what this means, but I know I don't like it." I appreciated the honesty and said so. The parable is offensive and scandalous, and it is intended to be. What kind of religious leader, let alone savior, tells stories like this? What kind of God is this? God should be just and fair, right?

The parable is designed to get us to identify with the all-day workers, and we usually oblige. We see ourselves as those who have played by the rules, worked hard and long, and deserve what we have. Like the all-day workers in the parable, most of us aren't happy when we don't get what we feel we deserve, or when life doesn't operate on a strict calculus of rewards and punishments according to merit.

But what if that's not who we are, and not where we are in the lineup at the end of the day? What if our flattering picture of ourselves isn't the true picture? What if God sees us not as the all-day workers but those who have arrived late and been paid generously? What if we have not gotten exactly what we deserve, but more, much more than we deserve? What if we have been the recipient of breaks and blessings all along the way? The parable asks, What if God, or life, is not fair but gracious? Suppose we all have gotten more than we deserve and that we are all recipients of amazing grace and generosity?

Like so many of those Jesus told, this parable is not a solution to our problems; it is a problem to our solutions. It challenges the ways we have come to think of ourselves as deserving of all that we have because we have earned it and consigned others to the category of undeserving. It messes up our world, and the little account book that most of us carry somewhere in the back of our minds. It does this in order to give us a new world. We are not the deserving or the entitled. We are the graced and the blessed. Life is not our due and certain benefits are not our right. Life is a gift and to live it is grace. Jesus is the problem for our solutions.

I tell my students that the parables are like hand grenades. They are intended to blow up our world, our explanations of how things are. Often the problem is that we preachers throw our bodies on the explosion to protect the congregation. We domesticate the parables and the gospel, adjusting them to our world rather than letting them transform people to a new world. When we explain the parables, we often explain them away.

Not only do we often turn religion into the solution for our problems, and thus miss its transformative power, we often miss the element of paradox at the heart of Christianity. We have reduced it into sensible little maxims like, "God helps those who help themselves," "It is more blessed to give than to receive," and "Do unto others as you would have them do unto you." We nod in agreement and go on unscathed. Not so with the Gospel's paradoxes.

Consider the Sabbath paradox. Most everyone today seems not to have enough time. "There's never enough time to get everything done," we complain. "I am constantly busy, way too busy," we moan. Of course, if someone phoned and asked if we were busy and we said, "No, I'm not busy," we might be thought of as odd or even as un-American. "No, I'm not busy." "You're not busy. Is something wrong?" Still, we complain of it. The Gospel paradox for this one goes like this: "You're too busy? Here's what you do. Take a day off, a full day, one full day each week, completely away from work. For one day a week do nothing, nothing but dream, pray, and rest. Take naps, make love, go for a walk. Lie on your back and look at the clouds. It is the only way to have enough time, to take off a complete day, a day off every week."

We say, or think, "An entire day. I can't possibly take a day off." This paradoxical faith says, "You can't possibly *not* take a day off." Without a complete day devoted once a week to doing nothing, you will become lost and confused. You will think it is you who made the heavens and the earth and that everything depends on you. You will think you are Atlas, the Greek god, who tried to carry the entire world on his shoulders. Stop it, right this minute. You're not *that* important. "Finish your work and take a day off!" "But I'll never finish my work. My work is never done!" we protest. Then, said the rabbis, "Rest, *as if* all your work were done." The difficult thing here is that we live in a 24/7 culture (and proud of it too!) so that you need to find friends, companions, if you're going to pull off this countercultural activity of rest, of Sabbath, of doing nothing. Most of us don't have the strength to manage it on our own.

The Gospel teaching about money is equally odd and paradoxical. How will we ever have enough? Just when we think we have enough, college tuitions soar. Just when we imagine we've saved enough for retirement, yikes, we may live to be 103 and require twenty-four-hour care for years. And then there's keeping up with the Joneses, and getting that new stove that looks and sounds like a rocket launcher or the new car that wheels around like our own private tank. How will we ever have enough? The chant is ever in the background, and sometimes in the foreground: "Never enough, never enough," though we live in the most affluent society on earth in the most affluent time in history. Here's how to have enough. Give it away. I promise it's the only way to have enough. Give it away, 5 percent or 10 percent or more, and take it off the top, not the bottom. It's the only way you'll ever be free. It is the only way you'll ever have enough.

Then there's the one I think of as the Lenten paradox: "Less is more." Lent is a season of fasting and denial for Christians, giving up things like food or alcohol or television or complaining. It is not so much about deprivation as it is to discover that less can be more, that in doing or having or consuming less we experience more, more of life, more of God. The wisdom of the culture goes by on trucks for some big-box store bearing the slogan "More of Everything!" That is our answer, not just materially but often spiritually. What we think we need is to do more, be more, accomplish more. Personally, I'm not so sure. I wonder sometimes if we are so hell-bent on more because we have no real clue about the why and wherefore of our lives. Lacking a sense of purpose, we fill the schedule. "Less is more" may be the timeliest of the great spiritual paradoxes.

If that is true, a close second must be the one about how to find yourself. We live in a society where we are forever talking about finding ourselves, getting in touch with ourselves, and being ourselves. And it is a challenge, no doubt about it. The crowning paradox of the Gospel is the central theme of Jesus' teaching, "Those who find their life will lose it, and those who lose their life for my sake will find it" (Matt. 10:39). "Can I find my life, my self, by losing my self? That can't be. It makes no sense." Right, it doesn't. And yet meaningful and fulfilled lives all over the planet and throughout history testify that it is true. Only in giving ourselves, losing ourselves, do we truly find ourselves. Only by forgetting ourselves do we remember ourselves.

In so many ways and places we seem to be experiencing what mystics have called "impasse." We have ground to a halt, unable to see a way through or around or over the challenges and impasses before us. We apply our linear, rational, problem-solving minds and methods and somehow it gets worse, not better. Our vaunted solutions create new and unanticipated problems. Working harder doesn't make it better, it only makes us exhausted. We experience ourselves as somehow caught. "A genuine impasse," writes theologian Belden Lane, "is such that the more action we apply to escape it, the worse it gets."[7]

Enter the counterintuitive, the provocative, and the evocative. Come now the prophet and the poet. Enter the parable and the paradox. Call forth the problems for our solutions. By such as these shall light be shed upon our darkness and the way ahead revealed to us.

# BEWARE OF
# PERFECTION

I HAVE OFTEN HEARD it said, usually with great bravado and gusto, "The good is the enemy of the best!" These confident speakers maintain that we should strive for the very best and not settle for the merely good. Of course, if we're speaking of tuning up a car and the *merely good* means connecting three of the four spark plug wires, I would agree that only the best will do. But usually we're not speaking of such clear-cut matters. We are speaking of the less measurable circumstances of life, of persons, families, and communities. In these areas the fevered search for perfection can take on a harsh and a self-deceiving face. Some parents drive their children, and themselves, so relentlessly toward achievement and perfection that all joy and playfulness, not to mention love, is wrung right out of life.

It seems notable to me that in the Genesis story of creation the repeated refrain as God the Creator works away at the six-day project is, "And God saw that it was good." Or, on completion, "And God saw that it was very good." Please note that it does not say, "And God pronounced it 'Perfect!'" You'd think that if God were doing it, perfection might be the standard and the result almost by definition. But it's not. "And God saw that it was *good*." God seems content with *good*. One imagines a chirpy little motivational speaker, like an angry chipmunk, scolding God, "The good is the enemy of the best."

Why *this* refrain, "And God saw that it was good," and not "And God saw that it was perfect." Well, of course, because it is not a finished world. It's a good world, a stage for an unfolding drama, a work in progress. But it's not a finished world. Perfection and perfectionism labor under the illusion that we can attain completion, that we can get it absolutely right, and that we are in charge and in control. That's misleading and crippling. We are creature, not Creator. The Navajo remind themselves of this in every blanket they weave by allowing a mistake to stand. We are limited, flawed human beings. Perfection is not in the cards. Don't let visions of the best drive out the very good. I believe it was Augustine who said the only way to be perfect in this life is to know that you cannot be perfect in this life.

And it's OK. That is at least a good part of the message of the story of the temptation of Jesus, some version of which is found in each of the three synoptic gospels: Mark, Matthew, and Luke. Mark's version is terse and compressed, not saying much more than Jesus was driven by the Holy Spirit into the wilderness to be tested by the devil. Matthew and Luke offer more elaborate versions, each dividing the temptation into three separate episodes. In one, Jesus is offered power, all the power this world has to offer. In another, Jesus is tempted by great wealth and abundant possessions. In the third, the devil's offer is invulnerability. As they stand at the high peak of the Temple in Jerusalem, Satan says, "Throw yourself down; for it is written. He will command his angels [to] bear you up" (Matt. 4:6). Satan tempts Jesus to stand above and apart from normal human suffering and death, to be invulnerable. In a sense all three episodes are really about invulnerability, about escaping our finitude, whether through absolute power, infinite wealth, or divine protection. Each offers a kind of perfection, a premature completion of life grasped by us on our own terms.

Most of our ventures at perfection hunt smaller game. The perfect family. The perfect job. The perfect spouse. Perfect children. Perfect yards or gardens. Perfect looks and perfect bodies. The game may be smaller, but the hunt is still costly. It requires that we surrender our humanity and that of those closest to us. Moreover, it separates us from our brokenness and the brokenness of humanity.

The point of this temptation story is precisely that Jesus did not choose to stand apart and above our humanity or his own, rather he embraced it. He saw in our finite and limited humanity not a curse from which we must escape, but rather a blessing to be received. Unlike Adam, who reached out for God-likeness in Eden, Jesus refused to be other than human, other than finite and vulnerable.

This moment foreshadowed the rest of the story wherein Jesus embraced every depth humans may know. And yet by embracing his humanity and our own, with all of its perils, he also revealed its hidden promise. Hidden in our humanity is the promise of divinity. But this divinity is not the power to assert ourselves and dominate others. It is the power to give ourselves, to lose ourselves that we may be truly found. The poet Wendell Berry caught this paradox when he wrote, "We can make ourselves whole only by accepting our partiality, by living within our limits, by being human—not by trying to be gods."

Perfectionism tends, moreover, toward the tight and the uptight, toward life that ventures too little, lest we fall, lest we fail, lest we end up with egg on our face. Perfectionists don't get to laugh much, and they laugh at themselves not at all. OK, sometimes we shall fall and sometimes we shall fail. And then we shall return to the fount of grace and mercy whether we find it in a sanctuary or by a stream. It is seldom the end of the world. It might even be the beginning of a brand new one.

When I graduated from high school my minister gave me a page with a quote attributed to the Renaissance Christian Erasmus. I now give it to other young people at about the same stage in life. It is a blessing for the journey ahead and an emancipation proclamation from the bonds of perfectionism.

> *'Tis a brave world, my young doctor!*
> *Do not be afraid of it; do not calculate*
> *Your chances so closely that you miss your chance;*
> *Do not pretend to know what you do not know.*
> *Work and laugh and give thanks,*
> *For these three are one.*
> *You did not make the world.*
> *You cannot remake it.*
> *You cannot even spoil it.*
> *You may, however, know the wonder of*
> *Improving some small corner of it,*
> *But (do not forget that) before you arrived*
> *The World was pronounced "very good."*
> *Go now and enter its joy.*

# THE OTHER FACE
# OF PERFECTION

WHEN MY DAUGHTER was between ages six and eleven she played on a girl's soccer team that seldom won a game. And it didn't matter. At least that's what the coaches and the parents all said. "Oh, it doesn't matter," "Great game, you played so well," we told the kids as the team went down to another defeat and we passed out the snacks. Maybe at ages six and seven winning doesn't matter and shouldn't. Maybe just playing or even scrimmaging is quite enough. But I wondered if that were completely true. I wondered if it were a good idea to chirp, "You played so well," when they had not.

As the years went on I noticed things that suggested winning did matter. The girls were casual about showing up for practice. There was a cattiness among them, a backbiting, that suggested some unhappiness, something not working. They showed increasingly little respect for, or even attention to, their coaches. Meanwhile, girls who actually seemed to want to win, who took the competition seriously, and who played with some energy and determination, seemed odd and out of place on the team. "What's her problem?" was often heard about those girls. At the end of the year everyone got trophies: win or lose, show or no-show, trophies all around. But the trophies meant little to the girls perhaps because there was nothing to aspire to, no standard of excellence, and no expectations of playing well or as well as they could.

While I've been known to earnestly press the warning "Beware of Perfection," my message here walks the other side of the street. Beware the perils of going limp and lax, having no ideals or standards, no expectations. We struggle with our dual nature, both finite and free. We must learn to accept our limits and our finitude. "The only way to be perfect in this life," said Augustine, "is to know that you cannot be perfect in this life." But we are not only finite, we are also free. Our freedom means having ideals and aspirations. If at times we nod and say, "Well, she's only human," we ought also (and more often than we do these days) stand back and say, in awe and amazement, "What a thing a human being is!" I know that holding the two sides together is not easy, not simple. But then life's not simple, not really.

When my daughter was playing soccer and in elementary school, Seattle seemed a haven for the excesses of the self-esteem movement. Every childhood work of art was brilliant. Every writing venture was wonderful. Every child was brilliant and wonderful all the time, or so they were told. I couldn't help but wonder if this was helpful, let alone honest. What might become of children who had only ever been told that their every venture, thought, and expression was wonderful, brilliant, and terrific? The idea was that they would feel so good about themselves that they would be happy, healthy, and productive. But I was not so sure. I worried what might happen to children who were given the impression that the world revolved around them, that they would never hear a word of correction, challenge, or hard truth.

One can almost understand the "winning doesn't matter" philosophy and the focus on building self-esteem in young
children. But it is the extension of this one-sided and deceptive
picture into adult life and larger communities that becomes
problematic. It spills over in churches as well. Perhaps not in
all churches, but certainly in those I know best, the mainline
or liberal Christian churches. I have a friend who quips that in
these churches the sole measure and norm of Christian disci-
pleship is "being nice." "A failure to be nice," he says, "is really
the only thing that might get you thrown out." But this culture
of nice can often be a phony and quite fragile one, because it
fails to speak the truth, or as the apostle Paul enjoined it, "[to
speak] the truth in love" (Eph. 4:15). There's the challenge: to
speak the truth in love, whether in families, in the workplace,
in churches, schools, or community groups. Truth alone can be
cruel. Love alone can be cloying and, of course, not really love
at all. Together they balance and correct one another and make
life in community not only possible but desirable. Together
they offer a standard, a norm to which we can aspire, and an
expectation without which life goes limp.

Another aspect of this general drift is seen in grade infla-
tion in high schools and college. It's not hard, but rather easy
for teachers to dish out all A's to their students, or at least all
A's and B's. There will be few complaints. What's hard is to
make the grades mean something. What's hard is to give out
some C's and D's, if that is what has been earned and is merited.
With C's and D's a teacher can count on complaints. You will
hear from grumpy, disappointed students. You will hear from
their parents, and it won't be fun.

The theological term for this failure to hold ourselves
to some norm and standard is *cheap grace*. If *grace* is God's gift
of love, mercy, and life, poured out abundantly, *cheap grace* is

receiving the gift but without any subsequent change in one's way of life or behavior. Dietrich Bonhoeffer, who was martyred by the Nazis, did as much as anyone to popularize the term *cheap grace*. He charged that many German Christians and the German churches were happy to claim the name and perceived benefits of being Christian but without their faith asking anything at all, or at least anything remotely costly. Only cheap grace could allow German Christians to be complicit with Nazi atrocities.

Bonhoeffer believed that God's grace comes at a price. It requires a response, a new way of life, one that stands with those who suffer and the victims of injustice and oppression, even if it also makes you a victim, as in Bonhoeffer's case.

Today many of the churches of my own family of faith and tradition describe themselves almost wholly in what I think of as "soft" words. Words like *inclusive, open, affirming, diverse*, and *welcoming*. Nothing wrong with those words, of course. We ought to want churches to be all of these things. But the rub is that this is all many churches seem to be or aspire to be. They welcome people, but to what? Is there any specific Christian life? Is there anything challenging? Such churches are, to be sure, open. But doesn't openness lose its meaning if there isn't something to which one is closed to or at least averse to, some point at which a line is drawn?

My hunch is that churches, parents, and schools that speak only in low-demand positives and strive to be unfailingly nice and never to offend aren't very compelling, not even very interesting in the long run. Moreover, they do not serve their members well. I note with interest the large number of people and the high degree of enthusiasm in contemporary society for extremely demanding types of sports as well as craft and art forms. Think of rock climbing with its skills and its risks, for heaven's sake, or all the folks who train for and compete in marathons or long-distance bike rides and races. There are quilting groups and potters studios. The willingness of people to pursue such ventures, at some considerable cost in time, money, and effort, is remarkable. And then there are those who devote their lives to master a musical instrument or compete in a team sport. We crave challenges, and if they are not available in our prosperous and affluent culture, we will even try to invent them.

When performing a wedding I will often say something to the effect that marriage is a spiritual practice and discipline as demanding and as rewarding as any. People seem to become more alert when I say something like that, perhaps relieved to hear and hit upon something hard amid the fluff and fancy of the usual wedding. "Marriage won't be easy," I say, "but it can be good. It can be very good." What's challenging about marriage is what's challenging about life: paying attention to someone and something other than yourself, practicing forgiveness, hanging in there when it's difficult, and learning that strength is not so much the capacity to prevail as it is the capacity to bend, to bend without breaking.

More than any other of the Gospels, the Gospel of Matthew is devoted to the topic of cheap grace, to naming it and overcoming it. In parable after parable the Gospel of Matthew shows us those who have received a great gift, who have been forgiven an impossible debt, or entrusted with a precious house or estate. Over and over again, a moment of judgment comes, a moment when the receivers of a gift bury it rather than use it, when forgiven debtors do not extend forgiveness to those indebted to them, and when servants left in charge of the property let it go to rack and ruin. These moments of judgment always come as a surprise. And you can almost hear these characters say, "We thought you forgave all, accepted all, that whatever we did was fine." Or as the nineteenth-century German poet Heinrich Heine famously quipped, "I love to sin; God loves to forgive. Really, the world is admirably arranged." No, says Matthew's Jesus, something is required. Grace requires a response.

An entire school of sociologists of religion called the Rational Choice School has reviewed American religious history and reports that when churches lower the level of expectation for their members, when they ask little or nothing, they decline. It may seem counterintuitive to find that high expectations result in better response. But, in another way, it does make sense. When we know that something is expected of us, we tend to rise to the occasion. Many of us can recall that our very best teachers were seldom the easiest or even the most popular. Often they were grumpy, hard-edged, and demanding. And we loved them.

In the movie *A League of Their Own*, about the first women's professional baseball team, the team's star pitcher, played by actress Geena Davis, tells her coach, played by Tom Hanks, that she is leaving the team and going home. She's tired of the pressure, misses her husband and family, and is weary of the hoots and catcalls from the fans. "It just got too hard," she tells her coach, who is struggling with an alcohol problem but sober for the moment. His response is, "It's supposed to be hard. If it wasn't hard, everyone would do it. It's the hard that makes it great."

The great challenge is always to hold the tension of polarity, that is, to keep judgment and mercy in conversation, to hold together justice and forgiveness. It is never an either/or, but always a both/and. When we say, "Oh, it doesn't matter," or "Great game" when it wasn't, we lose that tension. On the other hand, when parents stalk the sideline, barking orders, criticisms, and demands, we have lost the tension on the other side—judgment snuffing out mercy. In parenting, in coaching, in teaching, and in life, the hard thing is to hold the two together, both expectation and mercy, both justice and forgiveness.

# SUFFERING

I WAS IN MY sixth period geometry class when word of President John F. Kennedy's assassination abruptly crackled from the school's PA system. What I remember most was the silence, the silence that suddenly framed and held all our words. That silence was not broken but deepened when our teacher, after some moments of his own stunned silence, said, "Let us pray." There has to be some silence around suffering. Easy answers, glib statements have no place.

And yet, in the face of suffering and evil we do search, if not for answers, then for meaning. Suffering tends to challenge the ways we have put life together. Suffering challenges our sense of meaning, and somehow we need to make some sense of it. As I think over the different ways that suffering is under-stood and explained in the biblical tradition, I see four different views, most of which are also reflected in different ways and words in more secular understandings.

One view of suffering has a very clear expression in the book of Deuteronomy, Moses' long sermonic exhortation to the Hebrew people just before they cross the Jordan and enter the Promised Land. His warning is much like that of a parent: "If you obey . . . [the Lord's] commandments, decrees, and ordinances, then . . . [the Lord] will bless you in the land you are entering to possess; But if your heart turns away and you do not hear, . . . you shall perish" (Deut. 30:16-18). It has the advantage of simplicity. Virtue will be rewarded, while sin will be punished. This is probably the most popular way of coming to grips with suffering. It's nearly instinctive for people to believe that any suffering is a kind of punishment. We moderns tend not to like the simplicity and judgmental tone of this connection, but it is still pretty deep within us. We hear that someone has cancer. We say, "Oh, that's awful," and then a moment later add, "But you know, he never did take care of himself." "It's colon cancer?" "Well, he was very uptight, too intense." Sad as it is, we tend to see a judgment, a punishment in it nonetheless. The devil will get his due. Of course, it cuts the other way as well. We might hear that someone has a terminal illness and protest, "I just don't understand how this could happen to her. She's the nicest person I know!" Suffering is often understood and explained as a reward or a punishment.

Not only is this way of understanding and explaining suffering apparently deeply rooted in us, there is an undeniable element of truth to it. More than we care to admit, we do bring trouble on ourselves, whether it is the smoking that brings on cancer, the one drink too many that leads to an accident, or the failure to pay attention to the hideous and hopeless social and political conditions that eventually flame forth in violence. There is some truth in this line of thought, but not the whole truth. It is at best a partial truth.

In a scheme in which suffering is understood as reward and punishment, the other side of the coin is, of course, that virtue is rewarded. Thus a life that is prosperous, healthy, and blessed with accomplishment and recognition must be a reward for good character. While there is truth in this, it's not complete truth, not absolute truth. As the prophet Jeremiah pointed out to God, and not very politely, the unjust prosper, while the virtuous suffer. The book of Job, moreover, is basically a book-length frontal assault on the Mosaic theory that virtue will be rewarded and that suffering is punishment. Job's erstwhile friends try to get him to confess his sins and fall into line with the conventional theology. "Surely, Job," they say, "surely, you must have done something wrong for all this to happen." Job won't buy it. He insists on his innocence, and in the end it is Job and not his pious friends who is vindicated by the Almighty.

Still, there is truth in the idea that virtue is rewarded and sin punished. It reinforces the idea of responsibility, and media personalities like Dr. Phil and Dr. Laura and Judge Judy are making a pretty fair living out of expounding this truth to a generation of slackers and cynics. "What were you thinking?" one can hear any one of this triumvirate question their willing miscreants.

The second view of suffering is, one might say, an elaboration on the Moses approach. It is the theory of suffering as character-building. If it hurts now, good news, it will be good for you in the long run. The apostle Paul seems to take this position in his Letter to the Romans: "We [boast] in our sufferings, knowing that suffering produces endurance, and endurance produces character, and character produces hope" (Rom. 5:3-4). There is also some truth here, I think. But it is probably a truth that people like to find out for themselves rather than have someone else point it out to them, especially when they're in the middle of the muck.

Suffering can teach us all sorts of things. We can figure out what really matters to us, and what we're willing to suffer for. Besides that, suffering can teach us what it is to be on the receiving end of help. Suffering can also show us how much we have in common with other people, most of whom have also known some form of suffering and sadness in their own lives. This last point highlights one of the great weaknesses of the theory that sin is punished and virtue rewarded. Those who are relatively well-off and comfortable or who have not experienced suffering often display a very unseemly smugness. A divorce, job loss, or an illness in the family can connect us to our fellow human beings in a way that prosperity and fair sailing often fail to accomplish, which is certainly an irony. There's no guarantee that suffering will bring people together, of course. Sometimes suffering turns people bitter, but less often than we might think. It was Hemingway who wrote, "The world breaks everyone; some grow stronger at the broken places."[8]

Still, this explanation of suffering can certainly become wooden when it is invoked too early, too often, or moralistically. "Now, son, this will be good for you" is generally not the kind of thing anyone wants to hear or really should have to hear. If it is the truth, we will figure it out on our own and in our own time.

The third explanation of suffering that emerges from the Scriptures is one Jesus himself articulates in the ninth chapter of the Gospel of John. In this passage, Jesus and his disciples have come upon a blind man who sat at the roadside begging. The disciples of Jesus wanted to have a little seminar on suffering and sin, and so they asked Jesus, "Who sinned, this man or his parents, that he was born blind?" (v. 2). They were working with the Moses framework, of blindness as a punishment for sin. The only question was, who was the guilty party? Who is to blame? It's a bit of a conundrum when the victim has been born afflicted. Jesus' answer is, in effect, "None of the above, and in fact that's not the point at all." He hastily ended the discussion, saying this was an

opportunity to do God's work of healing and giving sight to the blind, which he promptly did.

Jesus often bracketed out the questions of punishment, and blame, as he got on with doing something about suffering. Mother Teresa seemed to operate pretty much this way as well. She didn't spend much time or effort on trying to say who was to blame for the suffering and dying all around her. She just waded in to help. If the strength of the first interpretation of suffering is its emphasis on responsibility, the strength of the third kind of explanation is compassion. Suffering is an occasion for compassion.

In some ways, interpretations one and three reflect conservative and liberal politics, one leaning heavily on responsibility, the other on compassion. The fact that both views appear in the Scriptures suggests that neither is fully adequate or apt for all situations. The moral issue often hinges on sorting out the right balance of responsibility and compassion, of judgment and mercy. Either position, when taken to extremes or held too single-mindedly, creates problems.

Beyond that, the third interpretation, the compassionate response to suffering, has at least one clear advantage over telling someone "It's your own damn fault." That is, it combats or alleviates a frequent corollary or consequence of suffering, which is isolation. Sometimes the isolation is self-imposed, as when sufferers can't bear to be with anyone else or may think that no one else in all the world could possibly imagine what they are going through. Or sometimes people impose suffering on themselves as they interpret their problems as some sort of judgment, which renders them undeserving of company. Other times the isolation is imposed by others, especially when the only arrow we have in our quiver is the Moses explanation. If that is the case, we tend to shy away from sufferers, because whatever they've got might rub off on us. It is a well-known and sad fact that patients who aren't getting better usually see less and less of their doctors. If we can't fix it or solve it (read: control it), we're not sure we want to be around it. This is precisely where Jesus shook things up. He went to the incurable lepers. He hung out with the ne'er-do-wells. He crossed that line of demarcation. I've been grateful over the years that it is a pastor's job to go to and be with those who suffer. Left to my own devices I'm sure I would not have had the courage to do that. But as a pastor you have an excuse, even an obligation, to break in on the isolation, an excuse to be there, when sometimes presence is the only medicine we have to offer.

The isolation of suffering points us toward a fourth view of suffering that I find in the Scriptures, represented by one rather odd little story in the Gospel of Luke, chapter 13. Jesus was on his way to Jerusalem, where he would suffer an ignominious and painful death. At this time there had been two recent disasters with significant loss of life. The first was what theologians call an "historical evil": The Roman tyrant Pontius Pilate had recently sent his troops to slaughter a group of religious pilgrims who came from Galilee in northern Israel. The other disaster was of the type dubbed by theologians as "natural evil": For no evident reason a high tower in the city wall of Jerusalem (the tower of Siloam) had suddenly collapsed, killing eighteen people.

On the road to Jerusalem Jesus encountered a crowd that sought to query him regarding both incidents. He was a traveling rabbi. "Explain this," they said, "explain God's ways to us." As sometimes happens in stories in the Bible, Jesus put the words they were thinking in their mouths, or maybe they had said these things and now he repeated them back before answering. "Do you think," he asked the crowd, "that because these

Galileans suffered in this way they were worse sinners than all other Galileans?" (v. 2). "Or those eighteen who were killed when the tower of Siloam fell on them—do you think that they were worse offenders than all the others living in Jerusalem?" (v. 4). Then, sounding angry, he said, "No, I tell you; but unless you repent, you will all perish just as they did" (v. 5).[9]

On one hand, Jesus seems to deny their supposition that death and suffering is a punishment for sin, but then, almost in the next breath, he seems to threaten them with the very same thought. It is not easy to make sense of this passage and I'm inclined to think we ought not try too hard to make complete logical sense of it. What does seem true to me is that Jesus won't let those who have been disturbed and shaken by these incidents stop shaking anytime soon. If they had been able to say of the victims, "They deserved it, they got what was coming to them, they were worse offenders," as they were hoping to hear from Jesus, then they could have explained suffering and explained it away. They would have established a distance between themselves and those who suffered. They could go back to whatever they were doing, comforted in the knowledge that the awful thing that had happened to others couldn't and wouldn't happen to them. They would have restored their feeling of safety, however illusory it might have been. "Good thing we're not fools or zealots like them!"

Saying that, coming to such a conclusion is a way of protecting ourselves from the shaky feeling we have inside when suffering and tragedy strike, and that is precisely what Jesus wouldn't allow them to do. He didn't want them to run away from the torn place created by tragedy and suffering. Instead, he asked them to step into it. He didn't want them to fence off the crime scene or disaster area with a neat explanation. He wanted them to step through the fence and into the shaky place that the suffering has opened up in their own lives and hearts. He wanted them, and us, to do that because he knows that this torn place is also a holy place.

In this fourth view of suffering, there is no real explanation for it, except that it's a wake-up call. Wake up. Who are you? Wake up. Why are you here? Wake up. What are you making of your life? Those are holy questions, and Jesus does not seem to want that crowd of rubberneckers, or any of us, not to hear them, or when we do to run too quickly away from them. He wants us to feel the silence around suffering; the silence that happens when we don't have easy answers, or maybe *any* answers at all. In that torn place, says Jesus, there is a silence so deep that we may hear God speak.

In the end, of course, the Christian answer to suffering is the cross. But it is an odd sort of answer. It is not an explanation or a theory. It is a person and a presence. It is God's own embrace of suffering and sufferer. It is because of this, as much as anything, that I am a Christian. Suffering and sufferers are not judged, condemned, or rejected out of hand. The experience of suffering and those who suffered are embraced. As Dietrich Bonhoeffer put it, "Only a suffering God can help."[10]

# GET A WAY OF LIFE

YOU NEED TO be thinking about what kind of lifestyle you want in your retirement," said our financial planner the other day. He is a nice guy, a very nice guy. But what in the world am I doing with a financial planner? Or maybe I don't have him, maybe he has me. You're never really sure in such matters. True, he had been helpful to us in figuring out how to pay for college for our three kids, no mean undertaking these days. Someone who knew how to spin gold from straw would have been even more helpful, but since that service wasn't listed in the yellow pages we went with Larry, our "certified financial planner."

His question about our retirement lifestyle was jarring. Not quite like fingernails on the blackboard, more like the Christmas gift that makes you want to say, "This? This is who you think I am?" What was it exactly that so stuck in my craw? Maybe the implication that I was getting older? That certainly could be it, the source of my irritation. I always try to throw out the AARP membership applications that come in the mail with my name on them before anyone else notices them. Or possibly, it is the whole notion of retirement? Not me, I am in the prime of life. While both were, I confess, a little galling to me, it was the word *lifestyle* that did it.

*Lifestyle.* Where did this word come from? What does it mean? It was this flimsy word along with its marvelously, and so transparently, euphemistic quality that did it. "You need to be thinking about what kind of lifestyle you want in your retirement." Translation: "How much money do you want?"

Lifestyle is life defined and decided by money, how much of it you've got, and what it can buy. Somehow I find it difficult to imagine a poor person speaking of his or her lifestyle! But there's more than just the reduction of life to things. Lifestyle is part of the notion that identity is merely a matter of personal choice. We often hear people speak of inventing or reinventing themselves. "You can be a whole new you!" promise various advertisers. Someone is *into* this or that lifestyle. When you hear such things you can't help but wonder who someone or anyone is really, and will they still be recognizably themselves a month or year from now? Or will they have changed their lifestyle and become someone new and different, rather like a toothpaste or breakfast cereal? Somehow lifestyle turns the self into a product or commodity, just another thing to be marketed, to be bought or acquired, sold or cast off because it is now passé.

Is there an alternative to the now ubiquitous *lifestyle*? My friend Martin tells this story. He and his family were driving in New York City, in the Bronx, when their car got a flat tire. The car, he discovered too late, was without a jack to change the tire. Moreover, there wasn't a pay phone in sight (obviously this took place before cell phones became a part of our lifestyle). In the neighborhood of their breakdown, tall apartment buildings loomed like fortresses.

Then a cab pulled over nearby and let out a little lady who was as stooped over as if she were carrying the burdens of New York on her back. Martin approached her slowly, so as not to seem threatening, and explained his family's situation. She invited him into her apartment to use her phone. When he entered her apartment he was introduced to two other stooped-over women. Martin called the towing service but found that the line was busy. He called every few minutes, and in between he had a chance to learn about the keepers of this oasis of human kindness. He noticed a sign on the kitchen door saying it was strictly kosher. He saw that the kitchen table was set for the Sabbath meal. One of the women kept saying, "I hope your call gets through before Shabbat (Sabbath)." Then it hit him. As observant Jews, they would not use the phone after the sun went down and the Sabbath began.

Now the phone calls had a new urgency. The sun was making steady progress and he was not. Finally, he asked, "Can the phone be used after the Sabbath begins?" His three new friends seemed to be startled by the question. One replied, "No, we will not make any calls and we won't answer the phone either." It was just that simple, and just as problematic for him, as that. Then, perhaps sensing his reaction, she asked, "Are you a Jewish boy?" When Martin said that he was not a Jew, but a Christian, all three women laughed and rushed to reassure him by saying over and over, "Oh, you can call. We can't, but you go ahead." They all laughed together. With that, the sun slowed and the call finally got through.

What my friend encountered there in the Bronx was not a lifestyle but *a way of life*. The three stooped-over women were not wealthy people. To speak of their lifestyle would have seemed odd, if not silly. But they had something better, something richer and more complex and even more interesting than a lifestyle. They had a way of life. Or, more accurately perhaps, their way of life had them. They were participants in an ethical and spiritual tradition thick with symbols, language, and practices of living. A way of life, made noble by the many who

have kept it, and which has itself ennobled the lives of its prac-
titioners. A way of life that gave the lives of the three bent-over
women a moral context and significance that will forever elude
a *lifestyle.*

I would reframe Larry's question, or suggestion, about the
lifestyle we wish in retirement. Instead of "You need to be
thinking about what kind of lifestyle you want in your retirement," I prefer to consider my way of life as a person who is
part of a particular faith and tradition, and in the years and
chapters of life still to come, and in my old age, live in a way
that is in keeping with that way of life. "What does your way
of life tell you about how you are to live during retirement?"
That seems to me a question that is both more interesting and
more promising.

# THE GENERAL DANCE

*THIS IS another letter to my daughter, Laura, when she was fourteen years old. This one is about worship, or "the general Dance," in Thomas Merton's phrase.* [11]

**D**EAR LAURA, DO you remember when you filled out the application for the Spectrum Program? You were ten then, I think. You were asked to describe a special interest of yours. You picked reading. You *are* quite a reader. You are hardly ever without a book, and often you seem to be reading three or four books at the same time.

What I found so interesting was the reason you gave that reading is important to you. "Reading gives me another world." That's a great insight, wonderfully expressed. And you are right. Reading can be like stepping through the wardrobe door into C. S. Lewis's land of Narnia. Suddenly, we're plunged into a different world.

For me, and I don't think I'm alone in this experience, worship is something like that as well. We step into a sanctuary, a chapel, or a cathedral, and it's a little like walking through the wardrobe door. There's music playing, different light and colors, strange words and stories. Not always, but often, I feel a presence. I am on alert.

Now this may sound far-fetched to you. Maybe going to church hasn't ever felt like this—yet. (Or maybe it has?) But as life goes on, as you become involved in all sorts of things and have the usual worries, you may one day find that worship *is* like stepping through the door to a different world, a world where we see ourselves and others, and even life, differently. A world where we are caught up in a special and wonderful story.

There is a danger in this. It's also a danger in reading, in play, and in all sorts of activities. The danger is that we step through the doorway into a different world and it becomes our hiding place. A place to escape from life and all its problems. Some people say that's all church and religion are—an escape or a hiding place for people who can't face the real world. And sometimes they are right. Church may become a crutch for some people.

I have told you that when I was a teenager I spent some time, maybe a lot of time, hiding. I was afraid, I guess, that people wouldn't or didn't like me, or that people would think I was dumb or that what I said was stupid. But sometimes I was afraid of exactly the opposite, not that people would *not* like me, but that they would like me *too much*. I felt that way about girls, who seemed to be interested in me years before I was interested in them.

It's not always bad to hide. Sometimes we need to step back and figure things out. I always thought tree houses were ideal for that. I built a tree house when I was a few years younger than you are now. For me, it was a sanctuary. At times worship has been that as well, a place to step back and figure things out, to regain perspective. But church and worship never let me stay there. Over and over in different ways, church has been a place of challenge. I have been challenged to emerge from my shell and make new friends. Challenged to try new things and to say what I thought. Challenged, sometimes, to take a stand. In fact, when I was a teenager, church was the place, more than anywhere else, that helped me come out of hiding, and to try my wings.

In your reading you may have noticed that there is a pattern to most stories. First the stage is set, the characters are introduced. The plot is developed. The characters interact, and some change. Finally, there is some sort of conclusion to the story, an ending. The same is true for worship. There is a pattern to it. While different churches have different ways of worshipping, and worship may vary somewhat in the same church from Sunday to Sunday, overall and most of the time there is a pattern to it. It's a pattern in four parts, or as the Christian mystic Thomas Merton called it, "the general Dance."

The first part of worship is praise or adoration. Our attention is shifted off ourselves and onto God. Sometimes there is a rousing hymn, or the organ plays in such a way that it feels as if we are in the presence of something large and wonderful. Or we say words of praise, or whisper a prayer of adoration. Though no one ever says it just this way, it's all about forgetting yourself. I like very much the way Merton puts it: "The fact remains that we are invited to forget ourselves on purpose, cast our awful solemnity to the wind and join in the general Dance."

The second movement in worship is confession, confession of who God is and who we are in relation to God. Sometimes confession happens in words, sometimes in silence. Other times it's a song. Before the holiness of God, we say what is true about ourselves, that we haven't lived in true and holy ways. The third big movement in the general Dance is a word from God, usually in the form of a scripture reading, a sermon, and the sacrament of Communion. (Every now and then in the Bible God says to someone that it's not enough to just hear the Word, you need to eat it, chew on it, swallow it, and take it into yourself, which is a way to think about Communion.)

And then in the fourth and last movement in the Dance called worship, we are blessed and sent out. Sent off into life and the world to take our place there as co-creators with God, and to tell God's story of love, truth, and mercy for the whole world. Those are the four movements, the four steps in this Dance. In different churches they do them in different ways. Some kneel. Others stand. Some sing. Some chant. Some tear hunks of bread off a loaf, while others eat thin little wafers. Some ministers shout and sing when they preach. Others talk quietly. But the four movements, the four steps of the general Dance are usually there: giving praise, saying confession, hearing the Word, being blessed and sent out into the world.

Have you ever noticed how going into the sanctuary in our church could be thought of as something like going into a womb? The sanctuary is rounded, and you go in by going through a hallway that could be thought of as a kind of birth canal. And at the entry point, just before your eyes are drawn up by the stained glass and light shining in, there is the baptismal font, full of water.

Going to worship is a little like going back to the womb, back to where we are dependent on something or someone else. We rest, as an old spiritual puts it, "on the bosom of Abraham." We all need that at times in our lives, no matter how old or how grown-up we are. But we don't get to stay there. We get re-birthed, reborn, and sent back into the world to stand on our own two feet and be independent. That is the rhythm of this dance and of the life of faith. Back and forth, in and out.

Dependence and independence. Tending to our roots, spreading our wings. We need both.

As you wrote of reading, "Reading gives me another world," likewise I think of worship, with its four parts. It gives us another world, another story. The great story of God and God's persistent and costly love. When we go back into the ordinary world, we aren't quite the same. We have been changed, at least a little, transformed by a different world and a different story. And, who knows, having learned to dance in this way here, we may just break out dancing to the Lord in all kinds of places?

*Love, Dad*

# CHRISTMAS

WHEN ALL THE gifts have been unwrapped, and the feeling "Is that all there is?" begins to creep in like a chilly fog, and you're not sure what to do next, read the story. Read the actual Christmas story—that is, not Dickens or Clement Moore or Peanuts, but the real one. The real Christmas story, of which there are two in the New Testament.

Unless you are pretty familiar with the Scriptures, you may be puzzled. "Two Christmas stories?" you may be thinking. "What do you mean by two? I thought there was, you know, *the* Christmas story, the one Christmas story."

Recall, there are four Gospels, four stories of good news (*Gospel* means "good news") about Jesus. These are the Gospels of Matthew, Mark, Luke and John. Of the four only two have stories of the birth of Christ. By now, you may have a different question, namely, "If there are four Gospels, why aren't there four Christmas stories?" Good question, no easy answer.

Perhaps Mark and John passed on the birth story because they had a sense that the Christmas thing might get out of hand, as it surely has. Mark starts right in with John the Baptist calling people to repent and "Prepare the way of the Lord!" (Mark 1:3). John creates a prologue as majestic and haunting as the creation story in the first chapter of Genesis. It falls to Matthew and Luke to include the story of the birth of Jesus.

But, one more surprise, their two Christmas stories are quite different.

The differences between the two, between Matthew and Luke, have given skeptics a lot of ammunition. Behold the contradictions! they said. But the differences are contradictions only if you are operating with a modernist's notion of truth, which is that truth is only what actually happened and can be verified by empirical data. To be sure, that is one kind of truth, but not the only one nor perhaps even the most important one. There are other kinds of truth and the Gospels offer us these. Though they are grounded in history, the Gospels offer not so much historical truth as theological truth. That is to say, the truth they offer is not the "Just the facts, ma'am" preferred by police sergeant Joe Friday on *Dragnet*. Rather it is the truth of meaning. What does it mean? Luke and Matthew have different Christmas stories because they seek to convey different meanings and different truths. And that is the best answer to the question of why Mark and John do not have Christmas stories. They sought to convey other meanings, other truths.

This notion of truth is what the novelist Thomas Mann had in mind when he described and defined *myth* as "That which never was, but always is." The Native American shaman and storyteller Black Elk made the same point when commenting on the truth of the stories of his people: "Whether it happened so or not, I do not know; but if you think about it you can see that it is true."[12]

The best-loved and best-known of the two Christmas stories is found in the Gospel of Luke, chapter 2, the first fourteen verses. You might say this is a "Christmas classic," sort of like Coke Classic, only not so sweet. That's OK, after all the cookies and candy and spiritual sentimentality, you're probably in the mood for something that's not so sweet.

To be sure, there is the sweetness of a child's birth. But it is bittersweet, for as Luke tells it, "there was no place for them at the inn" (Luke 2:7). This wasn't just a failure of parental planning ("But Joseph, why didn't you make a reservation—you knew Bethlehem would be crowded!"). Nor is it merely an interesting but inconsequential footnote. It is Luke's way of telling us that even from his birth this much was already clear: The world would not receive him. There was no room. No vacancy. We are, you see, too full, too full of ourselves. If you want to welcome him, empty and hungry is how you have to be, or at least Luke thought so. Desperate is good too.

Still, God is not deterred by our "No Vacancy" signs. God decides to come anyway. As they like to say in African American congregations, God finds a way when there is no way. Moreover, God's way is not one any of us would have thought of, which is also the point and the truth. The child, God's own child, will be born out back, in a manger. *Manger* may sound nice, but probably it wasn't. Probably it was darn cold and smelly to boot. And yet, it is amazing how bright and warm almost any place can be when real love and true humility are found there. That truth is one of the small good things of which this story, the Real Christmas Story, reminds us.

It is Luke who puts the shepherds on the Christmas stage and in the spotlight. But there are more surprises here too. These shepherds aren't who we think they are. They were not rustic, romantic, salt-of-the-earth, saints of yore, appropriate for Christmas cards and lovely living manger scenes complete with choirs. They were ne'er-do-wells and outcasts, guys who worked strange shifts and were mostly invisible in the daylight. Because of their work they weren't able to keep up with the various rituals and requirements that made a person ritually pure and socially legitimate. Remember the "no room" thing; God has a hard time with those who are full up with their own virtue and importance, but those without much of a resume, i.e., shepherds, will do fine.

Back then, decent people snubbed shepherds much like most of us snub their contemporary cousins, the night watchmen and the janitors, the truck drivers who drive through the night, or the homeless men warming themselves around a burn barrel beneath a bridge. Still, they were God's idea of a good time. From the get-go, it seems that Jesus kept company with the wrong kind of people!

Matthew's version of the Christmas story has never been quite as popular as Luke's. Matthew is neither the artist nor the storyteller that Luke is, but there's another thing too. Perhaps Matthew didn't win the Emmy because he somehow forgot to actually include the story of the birth itself. A curious oversight for a birth story, I'd say. Although Matthew leaves out the actual birth, he does manage to give us, in his first chapter, a genealogy of forty-two generations, which begins with Abraham, runs through David, and culminates in Joseph. But if Joseph's not the father, why bother? Because however unexpected or unconventional the method (and a careful study of the genealogy will reveal both) God is making good on a promise, a promise made long ago and far away to the ancestors. When we see no way, God finds a way. Same song as Luke, but different verse. A different way of conveying the same message: the message of grace.

Joseph figures as prominently in Matthew's Christmas story as Mary does in Luke's. (Please note: Long before historians thought to write "women's history," the Scriptures give us this story from a man's point of view in Matthew and a woman's point of view in Luke!) You'll find Matthew's version in chapter 1, verses 18-25, with a second act in the first 12 verses of chapter 2. Joseph, at center stage in act one, is the patron saint of every man or woman who has had to overlook a rather major personal slight to get on with what's important and do the right thing. Joseph was not the father, but Mary needed him, and God did too, and he stuck it out, despite his better judgment. Sometimes doing the right thing may look completely wrong.

Joseph would have been right, and within his rights, to send Mary packing, even to have her stoned as an adulteress. But Joseph had no instinct for revenge. He was prepared to dismiss Mary quietly, saving as much of her honor as he could while doing what must be done under such circumstances. That was the plan until a messenger in a dream told him what angels always tell us mortals: Do not be afraid! This messenger told Joseph, "Do not be afraid to take Mary for your wife, for . . . she will bear a son, and you are to name him Jesus, for he will save his people from their sins" (Matt. 1:20-21). Well, at least Joseph got the naming rights. So Joseph gathered his courage and did as told, though it meant he did the "wrong," that is, the unlawful, thing.

In Matthew's act two, wise men arrive from the east, probably from what we know today as Iraq. If part of what Matthew wants us to know is that God keeps his promises to the tribal ancestors, he also wants to make clear from the start that this birth, and this life, isn't just for one nation or race, tribe or culture, hence the wise guys arrive from elsewhere, representatives of the rest of us. What I've always liked best about these very wise men is that they behave like nothing so much as kids. After all, they chase a star for hundreds of miles. Maybe the real wise people are those who haven't quite forgotten a child's capacity for faith and wonder and foolishness?

One of the implications of this quick review of the Bible's two Christmas stories is that the standard version—which slaps together shepherds and wise men, inns and stars, Joseph and Mary, Herod and Caesar into one extravaganza worthy of Cecil B. DeMille—is nowhere to be found in the Bible and *not* the real story. Pulling together such a mishmash of the two versions would be a little like lumping a couple of very different productions of Shakespeare into one gaudy and confusing blowout. Still, I know it may come as a shock that there are two real Christmas stories. But when the shock wears off, you may find the restraint and spareness of the originals to be a pleasing antidote to the general excess of the season. Read the Stories, the real ones. Read them slowly, carefully, lovingly.

# BLESSING

ONE OF THE great things about being a pastor is that you get to bless people. That said, I've never been a fan of the easy and sometimes (or so it has seemed to me) glib word of blessing. I'm thinking of the "God bless" uttered at the end of a pastor's taped phone message or the pontifical "God bless America" with which presidents invariably end their speeches. Such blessings always seemed to me like ketchup. Their general function being to smother what is otherwise unpalatable. Moreover, like ketchup, they are used without discretion, just slathered on everywhere and everything.

Mostly I have reserved the act and words of blessing for that closing moment in a service of worship called the benediction, also known in other settings as "The Blessing and Sending." After leading the congregation through the various movements of worship—adoration and confession, Scripture and sermon, prayers for the world and gathering at the table—then it is time for the blessing. I throw my arms up in the air, as if embracing God's flock, and then utter a good word, a benediction. It seems vaguely superstitious and ancient; on one hand, maybe a little threatening and yet on the other hand hopeful and promising, and quite loving.

The ancient and superstitious feel of benediction is probably based on the association of blessing with the time of death and the transfer of power from one generation to another. The "Bless you" spoken when someone sneezes harkens, I suppose, to an earlier time when the common cold, often a prelude to pneumonia, might easily lead to death. In the Hebrew Scriptures the patriarchs Isaac and Jacob, as well as others, confer a blessing on their often-competing offspring, and with their blessing comes power.

The French *Adieu*, the Spanish *Adios*, and the English *Good-bye* are all saying the same thing, "God be with you" or "The Lord is with you." A blessing spoken as we part company recognizes the uncertainty of the future and yet affirms a basic trust and confidence in life: God is with you. Your various comings and goings are somehow held, and you yourself are held, by a beneficent power. It is a remarkable and wonderful moment in a service of worship, and yet one that took time for me to appreciate and to sense its depths and power. No one ever said a word about it in seminary, which may be just as well.

The blessing I most often use is based on the so-called Aaronic blessing from the Old Testament's book of Numbers, chapter 6, verses 24-26. It has the power of something ancient and tested:

*The Lord bless you and keep you;*
*The Lord make his face to shine upon you, and be gracious to*
*    you;*
*The Lord lift up his countenance upon you, and grant you*
*    peace,*
*This day and forever more. Amen.*

The other blessing drawn from the Bible that I most like is based on one from Paul's Letter to the Philippians, chapter

4, verses 4-7. What makes this one especially powerful is that Paul was in jail, due to the Roman persecution, when he wrote the letter and its blessing. That is to say, it is no chirpy, positive-thinking or Pollyanna type of blessing, but hope born and kept alive in dark times and in shadowed places:

*Rejoice in the Lord always; again, I will say, Rejoice.*
*Let your magnanimity be known to all.*
*The Lord is at hand.*
*Have no anxiety about anything, but in everything,*
*By prayer and supplication with thanksgiving,*
*Let your requests be made known to God.*
*And the peace of God, which passes all understanding,*
*Will keep your hearts and minds in Christ Jesus.*

A bit long, perhaps, and not without some words that are a little hard to wrap the tongue around, like *magnanimity*, but that can also be translated *forbearance*, or even *graciousness*. The idea that we can or should have "no anxiety about anything" seems so completely impossible that it is also, in an odd way, wonderful.

Blessings come, of course, in contemporary language and forms as well. Perhaps the more contemporary of them will not stand the test of time, but that's all right. Some things live but for a season and are beautiful in their time. One new blessing that I especially like speaks what our society often refuses to acknowledge, namely, our mortality. From that acknowledgment derives a sense of urgency:

*Life is short,*
*And we do not have much time to gladden the hearts*

*Of those with whom we walk the way.*
*So be swift to love,*
*And make haste to be kind.*
*In the name of our companion on the way,*
*Jesus the Christ. Amen.*

Like that one, the next one also looks explicitly toward life
and living *after* the benediction, toward living as people who
know they are blessed and who are then to be a blessing to others. Not incidentally, that is the entire purpose of the church,
blessed to be a blessing.

*May God give you grace*
*Never to sell yourself short,*
*Grace to risk something big for something good,*
*And grace to remember that the world is now too dangerous*
*For anything but truth and*
*Too small for anything but love. Amen.*

A fifth and final blessing that I love is compact, even terse,
but extremely powerful. For me it conjures the spirit of such
great and courageous witnesses and martyrs as Augustine,
Martin Luther, Martin Luther King Jr., and Dietrich Bonhoeffer. In doing so it not only reminds us to keep first things first,
but also that the possibility of heroism is never as distant as we
might imagine.

*May you love God so much that you love nothing else too*
  *much;*
*May you fear God enough that you need fear nothing else at*
  *all.*

A tall order, to be sure, but in a world and society where life is so often cut to size and rendered trivial, it is both a blessing and an act of resistance.

These days, and as I write this, I have no congregation of my own, no flock to pastor, for the first time in twenty-eight years. And what I miss most, quite possibly, is giving the blessing.

PART TWO

# ON RELATIONSHIPS

# A PERSON IS A
# PERSON BECAUSE
# OF OTHER PERSONS

WE ARE ALL familiar with the African proverb "It takes a village to raise a child." Another proverb, of a similar spirit, comes from the Bantu peoples: "A person is a person because of other persons."

Fifteen years ago, when I stood up to preach my very first sermon at Plymouth Congregational Church in downtown Seattle, I said, "What you see standing before you now is a single person, one man. But that is not really the case. I am, if not surrounded, then at least shadowed about by countless others. There is my immediate family—my wife, Linda, and our three children, Joseph, Nick, and Laura—and beyond them a much larger family. There are my own parents and grandparents, as well as Linda's parents. There are aunts and uncles, nieces and nephews, in-laws and cousins. There are also the three congregations where I have been privileged to be a pastor and who have shaped me as a pastor and a person. For the congregation I've just left, I grieve my separation from them, and they grieve their separation from me, just as you grieve for your former minister. There is the church in which I grew up, its ministers, its Sunday school teachers and youth leaders. There are the schools I have attended, the colleges and seminaries, and my teachers and professors. There are countless other persons, neighbors and friends, coaches and authors, who loom large somewhere in the background. So you see, there's not just one man standing here, but a rather quite a crowd. And I understand that the same can be said for each of you sitting in the congregation today. Furthermore, something similar can be said of this church. As the author of the Letter to the Hebrews puts it, 'We also are compassed about with so great a cloud of witnesses' (Heb. 12:1, KJV), those who have gone before us in this life and in this place. A person is a person because of other persons."

Such an understanding of identity and what it means to be a person is at odds with much of modern and Western understandings of such matters, for which the ideal of the autonomous self prevails. Over the years Linda and I have attended two college orientations for our two sons. Both were at colleges that were originally founded by churches and shaped by religious aspiration. Both are now secular, with religion departments the only vestige of their origins. Sometime in the course of both orientations we heard college officials or faculty members tell incoming students something to this effect: "We are here to teach you to think for yourselves, not to accept ideas just because someone says that you should. You must make your own choices, determine and define your own values." At the second hearing of this confident pronouncement, I leaned over to my wife and said, "So, what else is new? These kids have been hearing that message their whole lives. It's the message of the entire culture." That message is "You are on your own. There's nothing you can count on, nothing beyond yourself that you can rely upon, turn to, or are accountable before." A friend of mine once observed that the story modernity tells is that we have no story.

We have no story except the story we choose for ourselves. But one might counter, Where did you learn *that* story, that idea? Who taught you, who told you, that?

When we push the notion of individual autonomy to such unquestioned extremes as is common today, we tend to lose perspective on the truth of our interconnectedness. We are a lonely and rootless bunch, looking deep within or in far-off places for something we have lost. In many respects, this doctrine of the autonomous individual is at the root of profound personal and social problems. It does not recognize or support the need for socialization or formation of the self. It locates reality deep within, and bends most everything to a single criterion of the self: "Does this work for me?" "Do I like this?" "Does it make me feel good?" But this is to take ourselves far too seriously. Moreover, it leaves us and our children vulnerable to the largely amoral but hugely influential and formative powers of media and consumerism.

Among the persons who have made me a person, and the person that I am, three stand out. One is my paternal grandmother, Victoria Moon Robinson. She lived the longest of my grandparents, which gave me the opportunity to know her best. Like my grandfather "Doc Robinson," her husband, Grandma Robinson was a licensed pharmacist. They operated pharmacies in eastern Oregon. She also played the organ for services at the funeral parlor run by my mother's parents, in the town of Enterprise, the country seat of remote but beautiful Wallowa county. Grandma Robinson was a bright, cheerful, and yet sharp woman. She did not suffer fools gladly. Though in her later years arthritis kept her in a large rocking chair, she was alert and engaged, informed about the news of the day.

When I was about age twenty and in college, I paid her one of my fairly frequent visits. She was then living in Portland,

Oregon, an hour from where I went to school. One of the reasons she was a guiding star for me was, of course, that she was completely in my corner. I was the apple of her eye, and I knew it. But this did not mean that she wouldn't set me straight should she see the need. On that particular visit I must have been altogether too full of myself, for after I'd yammered on a while she looked me in the eye and said, "Mister, don't you ever think that you are any better than anyone else!" It was like the slap of a Zen master, and it woke me up. Moreover, it stands as an example to me of holding in tension deep and abiding love and truthful challenge and correction.

A second person who formed me was John Wightman, the assistant minister at the church in which I grew up, Rock Spring Congregational Church in Arlington, Virginia. My family moved to Arlington from Oregon when I was quite young because my father had taken a job with the federal government. John was probably in his mid- to late twenties when he came to our church, and I was a teenager when I got to know him. At the time I was working on my "God and Country" award for Boy Scouts, and he agreed to work with me if I would start attending the church's youth group, which I did. This was the era of the civil rights movement and John got me involved by taking me with him to African American churches in downtown D.C. as well as to racially integrated church camps, which were not without controversy in those days. What I saw in John was a combination of attributes I particularly admired: he was smart and intellectually alert, but also compassionate and engaged. That was who I wanted to be, and his example had a lot to do with my choosing to be an ordained minister.

Among John's gifts to me was his almost casual confidence in my abilities. One incident stands out. A carload of us, John and maybe four teenagers, were driving back from a week's church camp in New Jersey. We were in his car, an old Rambler with a standard shift. Most everyone was tired and sleepy, including John. He asked if someone else could drive for a while. I said I would but that I didn't know how to drive stick shift. He said, "Oh, you'll get it," and disappeared into the back seat. We were on the New Jersey Turnpike and I was fine so long as we were traveling at about 60 mph and I was in fourth gear. But every time we had to go through a toll booth, it meant downshifting. So every twenty miles or so, our drive became a bumpy affair with some stops and restarts. But John was right, I got it, got it on the New Jersey Turnpike of all places. But what I got over the years of our relationship was *much* more, it was his confidence in me, a confidence and faith in me that I very much needed at that point in my life.

A third person who formed me came sometime later in my life, beginning when I was twenty years old and then in all the years since. Teruo Kawata was the pastor of my wife's Congregational Church in Honolulu when she was a teenager. Teri performed our wedding, and eight years later preached at my own ordination to the ministry. Since then he has been a presence in our lives and in my life as a minister. He preached at my installation at Plymouth, and served as my replacement during a six-month sabbatical, by which time he was retired. Teri was himself deeply formed by his own Japanese American and Christian parents in Southern California. But he was not only formed by his family and their faith, but by his experience of racial prejudice while growing up. During the Second World War, they were referred to as "Japs" and expected to vacate the sidewalk when white people came along. After the attack on Pearl Harbor, Teri and his family were sent to detention camps for Japanese Americans. Such profound experiences of suffering seem to elicit two broad reactions in most people: they can close us down, make us bitter, and destroy our faith; or they can open us up, make us more compassionate, and deepen our faith. For Teri, the latter has been true.

Like my grandmother and John, Teri also believed in me, which was a tremendous gift. He would regularly show up during my seminary studies, internships, and churches in my early ministry career. He was always interested to know what I was discovering, doing, and reading. He kept an eye on my career, sometimes from close up, sometimes from a distance. For all this I feel an enormous gratitude and sense of privilege.

Recently I found myself doing a series of talks in the St. Louis area. Before going there I heard from a woman, Susan King Forbes, who had been a member of my congregation in Hawaii twenty years before. Susan had become a "student-in-care," preparing for ministry and attending seminary during this time. While in St. Louis, I had dinner with Susan and her family, meeting them for the first time, and I visited her church. Over dinner she said, "I've told lots of other people this, but I'm not sure I've ever said it to you. You are the reason I am a minister. Before I came to Church of the Crossroads and heard you preach, I'd never seen much point in it, in Christianity and the church, I mean. But you were different. You had something to say. You made a difference in my life. I just want you to know that."

And the circle turns: We who have been formed by others become formative and influential in the lives of others and of a new generation. We are blessed by both experiences. "A person is a person because of other persons."

# THE BLESSED TRIAL: ON BEING A PARENT

Not long ago I was driving somewhere when an advertisement came over the car radio. The announcer's voice said, "Being a parent should be the most fulfilling experience of your life!" In the background the voices of crying and fighting children could be heard. Then came the description of a parenting skills seminar, and a pitch to enroll and discover how parenthood can be your most fulfilling experience.

To be sure, there are moments of fulfillment for parents. And it is also true that being a parent can be tough. I have taken comfort in my parental endeavors from the counsel of the poet and farmer Wendell Berry, who observed that "Parenthood is not an exact science, but a vexed privilege and a blessed trial."[1] Parenthood is, Berry continues, "Absolutely necessary and not altogether possible." These paradoxical observations seem to me to strike the right balance, the balance between a proper recognition of one's responsibility and a wise recognition of one's limits. Such a balance seems crucial to the vocation of being a parent.

In a society that is as confused and chaotic as ours appears to be, we will hear more about parenting skills seminars, and maybe even about such ideas as licensing parents. In the state where I live a woman recently dropped off her three-year-old at a freeway rest stop with the comment that she had "had enough." Such accounts, and many others that are much more incredible and brutal, come to our attention so frequently now that one response will surely be more parent education, more focus on developing parenting skills, and the like. It may even do some good.

Still, I wonder if developing skills and techniques and pushing more education—the American answer to most everything—is really what is needed. Or is the matter a deeper one? Perhaps being a mother or father requires not so much expertise and better parenting technique as self-understanding and wisdom. Perhaps being a good parent is more a matter of character and wisdom than of skills or the latest how-to manual or trends. But it is just this matter, of developing and sustaining a coherent sense of self and of character, that is such a challenge in our culture.

In Rabbi Edwin Friedman's book on families and family systems, *Generation to Generation*, the author discusses the relative merits of expertise, on one hand, and self-knowledge, on the other, to leadership. Friedman notes that often we think of leadership—whether in family, church, synagogue, or society—as a matter of possessing and deploying relevant expertise. But to the extent that we define leadership solely in terms of expertise, Friedman claims that none of us will ever feel adequately prepared for much of anything and least of all for being a mother or father. You can't know all that you need to know.

Instead of thinking of leadership, or parenting, in terms of expertise or skills, the rabbi suggests another way of coming at it. He believes that a person's capacity for self-knowledge and self-definition is the key quality. "What is vital to changing any kind of 'family' is not knowledge of technique or even of pathology but, rather, the capacity of the family leader to define his or her own goals and values while trying to maintain a non-anxious presence within the system."[2] In other words, it's not so much what you know as who you are. What is necessary for this self-definition and "non-anxious presence" as a parent? Can religious faith and religious communities help a person or couple develop and maintain this sense of themselves and this capacity for self-definition?

Many have noted the tendency of people to get involved in a church or synagogue when they become parents. Like others, I have muttered skeptically about those who are seemingly "doing it for the kids." Then I became a father. Many things happen when a person becomes a parent. The schedules change. Finding time alone, or as couple, is nearly impossible. Your time is not your own. Besides all that, when we become parents we may realize, if we are fortunate, that we are not God, that is to say, we may realize that we are not in charge, not in control. Not that we actually were before we had kids, but it was easier then to sustain the illusion.

The otherness of our children instructs us parents in the limits of our powers, even as the startling dependence of our offspring reminds us of our significance and responsibility to them. A new generation, whether gurgling and cooing as infants or strutting and stumbling about as gangly adolescents, signals even more forcefully than graying hair and stiff muscles our own eventual mortality. It may be that people turn often to religious congregations as they become parents not primarily for the children but really for themselves, even if they're not fully conscious of it. Perhaps at some deep level becoming parents tells us that we are not sufficient all alone or on our own for such an awesome task as raising a child. We require a larger framework of meaning. Moreover, we need other people. We need their examples, their wisdom, and their support. Such an awareness of one's limits is surely the beginning of wisdom for parents. I suspect that, paradoxically, Friedman's self-definition and "non-anxious presence" require trust in a source and framework of meaning beyond our selves.

But what do congregations offer parents as they try to cope with the blessed trial? When I baptize an infant I am often struck by the enormous number of meanings that weave through the experience. On one hand, parents are recognized in their new role and responsibility. Though as part of the rite we ask parents, "By what name is your child to be called?" they themselves are also getting new names—of Mother, of Father—or at least the first-timers are. We ask these newly named parents an impressive set of questions about their own faith, their commitments, and their intention to serve as models and examples to their children. To judge from what happens at this moment, the community clearly affirms that being a parent is serious business.

Some today discount the role and significance of parents. Parents themselves, particularly when their children move into adolescence, question their significance. "Do I/we still matter?" It can often seem that peer groups, coaches, or even pop culture through television and movies are ascribed greater importance than parents. But don't believe it. During their child's adolescence and well beyond, parents remain critically important as well as absolutely necessary. What we do and who we are *does* make a difference. So churches affirm this conviction at baptism, but not only this one.

At some point in the baptismal service the pastor will ask the parents to literally let go of their son or daughter. They hand their precious child over to the minister, probably not the first instance of "letting go" of one's child, but one that seems charged with meaning, in my experience. Letting go is also a part of a parent's vocation. So we practice it here, in the midst of the gathered community. We hand over our son or daughter and hear them named not as our product, possession, or achievement, but as a "Child of God" entrusted to us. Entrusted to us, not owned or managed or made by us.

Thus, even as parents are reminded in such a moment of their high calling, they are also reminded of their limits, of the limits of their powers and even of their responsibility. We parents need to be reminded that we aren't perfect, that we will as parents make mistakes, and that there is forgiveness and grace, even for parents. We need to be reminded by the letting go of our child in the sacrament of baptism that being a parent is a discipline, or maybe dance is closer to it, of knowing when and how to hold on and when and how to let go. To quote Wendell Berry once more, "Children, no matter how nurtured at home, must be risked to the world."[3] This dual awareness of parenthood's significance and its limits, of its responsibility and grace, seems to me essential to the self-definition and understanding required of a good parent.

Baptism is also a time when we are reminded of our need for others. I am sometimes asked to perform a private baptism. Almost always I refuse. We need the congregation and community involved in every baptism, during which it enters into a covenant with us parents to love, support, and care for the child or children. The extent to which both parents (or sometimes only one parent) often bear the burden of raising children pretty much isolated from the community in contemporary Western society would probably strike many other cultures across the world as odd, if not disastrous. We need others and so do our children. In time they will need mentors who are not their parents. They will need to witness a community trying to be one. They will need the institutions of our common life, schools, transportation, health care, and universities, to name a few. No one raises a child alone. No one should have to.

After the radio advertisement confidently proclaimed that "Being a parent should be the most fulfilling experience of your life!" I shuddered to think of the parents who, listening to this brisk assertion, quietly damned themselves for their perceived lack of success or happy fulfillment. Religious congregations and faith communities need to tell parents that while personal fulfillment or happiness may and probably will be part of parenthood, neither one is the point. Neither personal fulfillment nor my happiness are sufficient goals for parenting, or for life. Parents are called to be faithful—to themselves, to their children, and to the God who is the source of all life. If personal fulfillment is the only standard or the primary one by which we judge ourselves, it is too tempting to bail out, surrender, or give up. Our relationship with our children has more to do with fidelity than fulfillment, more with fulfilling a trust than with success.

Like most of what is truly worth doing or undertaking in this life, being a parent is not something for which we are ever fully or adequately prepared. It is a vexed privilege and a blessed trial, and not an exact science. It asks of us not so much technique as character, not so much expertise as wisdom.

# HYPER-PARENTING

WHEN MY DAUGHTER began her senior year of high school recently, we spent some time during the summer on the Great American College Tour. All in all she and I visited four colleges, which seemed plenty enough to me. But that fairly pales by comparison to the itinerary of a good friend of mine and his son. They stayed with us on the western leg of their visit to eighteen different colleges. Today the college tour, including its interview for the prospective student and information session for parents, has become de rigueur. Is this a sign of what Dr. Alvin Rosenfeld and his colleagues call "hyper-parenting"?

According to Rosenfeld, parenting is now "the most competitive sport in America. . . . If you can put a Harvard, Yale, or MIT sticker on the back of the BMW, you've won."[4] This "eyes on the prize" approach to college admission overlooks the fact that a third of those admitted to four-year colleges do not graduate four years later, and that at the most competitive schools various anxiety disorders—from bulimia to depression—are increasingly common, some would say epidemic.

The symptoms of hyper-parenting include the busy child. This is the over-scheduled child, who shuttles, or more accurately is shuttled, from one activity, class, or program to another with no downtime tolerated or allowed. Another symptom is out-of-control parental anxiety, expressed by near addiction to the latest "expert" advice. Moreover, hyper-parents are fairly driven to see their child achieve excellence in a sport, musical instrument, or activity, preferably by age seven. Reading by age three is also good. In reality, hyper-parenting skews the relationship of parents and children—children are turned into products and performers, and parents into managers and handlers. This accounts for the strange and strained relations between many parents and children, with parents resenting their children who do not appreciate "all that has been done for them," while children resent that their parents are always pushing them toward some goal.

My own pet theory about how we got ourselves into this predicament is that it's related to the smaller size of the contemporary family. Most parents are more anxious about their first child. My wife and I certainly were. But by the time parents get to their third or fourth, they are, if not wiser, then at least too tired to be all that anxious. No, you are wiser. Experience does help. But since many parents today have but one or at most two children, fewer children have experienced parents and the general level of anxiety has risen even as our whole society seems more driven and competitive.

In good American fashion, various Web sites and articles are now blossoming with tips for how to avoid hyper-parenting, which led me to wonder if anyone has become hyper about hyper-parenting? My hunch is that the problem is a deeper one than will be cleared up by naming the syndrome and giving yet another list of tips. Are there twelve-step groups for parents suffering from hyper-parenting? It is deeper because what seems to be happening is that the overly competitive, driven, and anxious ethos of much of adult society is simply filtering down, way down, down to womb and before with designer genes and genetic engineering.

In a spring 2004 article in the *Atlantic* I first caught sight of the term *hyper-parenting*. In that edition, author Michael Sandel argued "The Case Against Perfection: What's Wrong with Designer Children, Bionic Athletes, and Genetic Engineering." He suggests that a good part of what it means to be a parent is to be "open to the unbidden,"[5] that is, to what we cannot control. What a wonderful phrase: open to the unbidden. But it's not only a wonderful phrase, it's a skill and virtue for life and living. By our example we can teach our children the capacity to be open to the unbidden or we can teach them the foolish and self-defeating idea that they should be in control at all time.

"In a social world that prizes mastery and control," observes Sandel, "parenthood is a school for humility." It is true, our children stubbornly refuse, bless them, to conform to our expectations and desires as parents. The amazing challenge and gift of being a parent is to love, hopelessly love someone who remains other, who is him or herself and not me or myself. This teaches us to be open to the unbidden. Sandel goes on to say that "such openness is a disposition worth affirming, not only within families but in the wider world as well. It invites us to abide the unexpected, to live with dissonance, to rein in the impulse to control. A . . . world in which parents became accustomed to specifying the sex and genetic traits of their children would be a world inhospitable to the unbidden, a gated community writ large."

Parenting, like life itself, is a tricky business. Parents must chart a course that includes and moves between two kinds of love: accepting love and transforming love. The one affirms the being of a child and lets them be, while the other seeks their well-being and prods their growth. Hyper-parenting is an excess of the latter and a deficiency of the former. If some parents err by not asking enough of their children, others make the mistake of pushing too hard, asking too much. Finding the right balance is the key. But that is a key which hangs on the hook labeled *basic trust*. In other words, if we operate from, in Erik Erikson's phrase, "basic trust,"[6] then we are able to allow a child of ours the room to grow in ways that may surprise us. If, on the other hand, we have created a setting of "basic distrust," then we will be overbearing in our attempt to control all the variables and engineer the outcome.

Within reason, we certainly can and ought to offer both challenges and opportunities for our children, but not with the idea that we can or should control the outcomes, or that a child of ours is a product to be engineered or an achievement to be created. The idea that we are or should be in complete or hyper control is not only a bad one, it is really an illusion, that is, a falsehood. It is a bad one in that it erodes our respect for others and openness to them. Everyone has to fit our predetermined or self-interested agenda. To demand this of a child is a kind of violence.

But such excesses of control are also an illusion. It may be a comforting illusion, at least in the short term, but it is still an illusion. There's an old saw that goes, "Want to make God laugh? Tell him your plans." Life is full of the unknown and the unbidden. Our humanity lies not in gaining control over all such unknowns and contingencies, but in developing a capacity to respond to them, to rise to the occasion.

Our son Nick is a constant reminder of this. As a preschooler Nick was notable for his apparent tone deafness. I had never before heard "Old MacDonald Had a Farm" in quite the atonal quality that four-year-old Nick managed to give it from the back seat of the car one day on the way to preschool. "Oh well," I thought, "music shall not be his thing. That's OK." That was an example of accepting love, or at least an attempt at it.

Less than a decade later, when in middle school, Nick thought playing the trumpet would be just the thing, and so he signed on for junior high school band. His band teacher counseled, "Give it up, you'll never be a musician." But Nick persisted. And we provided him with private lessons in a bid to offer some form of transforming love. In his second year of high school he made it, by audition, into the high school jazz band. In his senior year he won the Louis Armstrong Award for best high school jazz musician. He went on to play lead trumpet in the college jazz band and continues today playing trumpet in a band that plays reggae, jazz, and hip-hop in frequent gigs around town. He is not likely to ever appear on MTV or *Austin City Limits*, but then who knows? In any event, he enjoys his music and the friends that it has brought him. Often I go to his gigs, remember the kid who couldn't get off B-flat for "Old MacDonald," and shake my head in wonder and delight. "Openness to the unbidden" not only prepares us, and our children, to deal with life's crises and tragedies, but also to its unexpected joys and gifts.

As I wrote this reflection on hyper-parenting, an article titled "Quick! Is Johnny Signed Up for Daydreaming?" came my way. Among other things it reports on a Greenwich, Connecticut, mother named Bobbie Eggers who sits down to dinner almost every night with her husband and three children, ages nine, eleven, and thirteen. They read together at bedtime and play board games. Clue is a favorite. To attain this remarkable experience, the Eggers family has dropped out of figure skating, horseback riding, fencing and hockey lessons, and other activities for their children. Don't worry, they haven't actually become reclusive, as they still are involved in choir, soccer, and the study of musical instruments. But they've cut it back to something that they can handle and which allows time for life as a family. It wasn't a painless transition, however, as Eggers reports having lost friends over her decision to take her kids out of some activities.

That the Eggers family lost friends as a consequence of limiting the whirl of activities seems both shocking and quite telling. It's not just any particular pursuit, activity, or sport that is at issue, but something deeper, a way of life and an understanding of being human. Ms. Eggers and her family seem to have threatened this way of life. It doesn't take much these days to be a troublemaker or a revolutionary. Punching holes in the schedule will do it. Daydreaming will too. Dean of admissions at MIT, Marilee Jones, admits that "Colleges have created mechanisms to crowd out the kids who are dreamers, to crowd out the kids who step off the conventional path. But what," asks Jones, "does it mean to have a nation of kids who don't know how to dream?"[7]

# BEING A GROWN-UP

WHEN WORD GOT around that I was leaving my position as pastor at Plymouth Church in downtown Seattle for a new venture as a freelance speaker, teacher, and author, something happened that I had not anticipated. A succession of people urged me to consider running for public office, in part I suppose because I had frequently commented on public issues in my Op-Ed column in one of Seattle's newspapers. My initial response to their somewhat flattering suggestion was to say, "But I thought you liked me!" Running for and holding public office these days seems like a tough way to make a living. My next line of defense was to explain that parish ministers get to go to lots and lots of meetings, and that I was looking forward to not doing that for a while. I imagined that public office, any public office, would entail as many, if not more, meetings than my previous endeavors, thus, "Thanks, but no thanks."

In the course of these conversations there was a sentiment and phrase used several times that caught my attention. More than a couple of those who were prepared to sacrifice me on the altar of public service said, "We need some grown-ups in office!" Which led me to wonder, what exactly does that mean? as well as a corollary question, what is a grown-up? Suddenly it sounded as if the song of the sixties, "Where

Have All the Flowers Gone?" had been replaced by a new one, "Where Have All the Grown-Ups Gone?" Could it be that after so many years of being exhorted to get in touch with our Inner Child, some are longing for those who have gotten in touch with their Inner Grown-up? What does this plaintive call for a few good grown-ups mean? What is a grown-up? Here are some of my hunches about what it means to be a grown-up, which may reveal something about the perceived shortage of same.

Grown-ups are people who understand "It's not about you." It is about something bigger than you. It is about some larger purpose or mission, project or vision. It is about the work. It is about some whole that is more than just the sum of the parts. The whole, the purpose, or the project may be any number of things: being a family, being a church, being a school, being a business, being a community or a country. There's something at stake that transcends me. "It's not about you."

While religious people think of sin in a variety of ways, one enduring definition among Christians is that sin is our tendency to mistake ourselves for the center of the world. No, say all the great religions, you're special, no doubt about it, but not *that* special. There is another, a greater reality impinging upon us, calling to us. There is that before which awe, reverence, self-giving, and self-transcendence are the right response. It's not about you.

It is quite true, of course, that not every larger goal or purpose is a worthy one or one that should command our loyalty or devotion. On many occasions throughout history ultimate claims have been made for partial goods or outright evils with unhappy, even disastrous, consequences. Neither the company, or the country, or the cash flow are God. But, then, neither are you. Despite sentimental rhapsodies to the contrary, children are not always sweet and loving souls of goodness. Children can be little tyrants. It is about them. Being childish is insisting that our wants and needs come first (and last). The capacity to know and affirm and live from the conviction that "It's not about you" is a crucial marker of grown-up-ness.

Another way to put this is to rummage around in the box of more or less lost or forgotten good words and pull out a couple dusty ones, like *duty* and *sacrifice*. Both have suffered neglect in recent times. *Duty* seems a grim and gray sort of word. *Sacrifice*, meanwhile, seems only a step away, if that, from some really terrible terms like *co-dependence*. It is not difficult to imagine someone who spoke too often or too readily of duty or sacrifice being referred these days for a psychological evaluation!

I remember being at a picnic when my children were much younger. I was pretty much constantly busy that day, either playing with them or watching out for them, or some combination of the two. When there was a break in the action I settled into a chair next to a thoughtful, single man, a teacher at a theological seminary, who happened to be gay. To me he said, "Being a parent is a sacrificial vocation." It was one of the most affirming things I've ever heard. An acknowledgment that there are some things, maybe many of the most important things in life, that are sacrificial, and that this is not some sort of personal problem one ought to get over, but rather a value to be honored and esteemed.

Sacrifice is, of course, a central theme in faith and in the Christian faith particularly. The idea that someone has sacrificed on our behalf is, nevertheless, one about which many today seem ambivalent. A variation on this theme is the oft-repeated sentiment of older adults, "I don't want to be dependent on other people," meaning, "I don't want others sacrificing on my behalf." Well, it seems to me that we are all in countless ways dependent on others and that is not, necessarily, a bad thing. Moreover, we are all the beneficiaries of someone's, or more likely many people's, sacrifices on our behalf. Rather than imagining that we can step out of the cycle of sacrifice, it may be preferable to share in it, sacrificing in our turn on behalf of others, as others have sacrificed in their turn on our behalf.

All of this is another way of saying that adults are people who know that the world doesn't revolve around them. They are people who have the capacity to give themselves to larger causes and projects, while not surrendering personal integrity or morality and conscience. Grown-ups are people who have the capacity for sacrifice on behalf of the next generation, as well as for goods that are part of a common good, or in the effort to meet challenges that are in the shared interest of the community or group.

Besides being someone who understands it's not, or not all, about themselves, a grown-up is someone, I imagine, who has the capacity on occasion to say something unpopular. Grown-ups are those who have the ability to say "No," or to say "This is wrong," or "Friends, I think we are fooling ourselves here," and to risk the displeasure that may come from doing so. A self-centered person seems to me unlikely to risk the disapproval or displeasure of others on behalf of values or principles that transcend their own self-interest. But just as genuine leaders have the capacity to tell us not what we *want* to hear but what we *need* to hear, so genuine adults have the capacity to say "no" to their children (but not only their own children), to risk disapproval and disaffection, to say something unpopular on occasion. My hunch is that children who do not have parents or adults in their lives who are willing and able to play this part, to say "no," may feel lucky in the short-term, but in the long-term they may feel otherwise. Being a pushover as a parent is a cop-out that leaves children wondering, though they may be unable to articulate it, where the adults are and if the world they inhabit is safe or reliable. Sometimes children actually want us to say "no" to some fevered request or looming possibility.

The art of being able to say something unpopular lies in doing it in such a way that those to whom you are saying it know that you still care about them and that you are in it with them. But never to be able to say the hard thing, the difficult thing, or to speak the truth that hurts before it heals, is to fail the grown-up test. The capacity to say what is unpopular is not, however, to be confused with two common but cheap imitations: the rant and the whine. The rant is self-indulgent, while the whine is self-justifying. Saying the hard thing, the difficult thing, is neither of those.

A third quality of a grown-up is the recognition that life is complex and even tragic. Every gain entails some loss. In this life we attain only proximate, not perfect, justice. Life's distortions and deceits are not easily brought under control of our little schemes for self-improvement, our prudent rationality, or our best intentions. Recently a young woman consulted me about sexual ethics, particularly sexual intimacy apart from marriage. She said, "So long as no one gets hurt, it's OK, isn't it?" I said I wasn't entirely sure when or what was OK in a lot of instances, but I was pretty sure that anytime there is real intimacy and something like love, someone getting hurt is part of what happens or at the very least an inherent risk. "There's no love without the risk, even the likelihood," I said, "that someone will be hurt. We can't escape that and we're kidding ourselves if we say that we can."

The trick, of course, is to look life's messiness, complexity, and tragedy in the face and not be undone or paralyzed by them. The trick is to dare to try, to hope, and to love, despite it all. A conscientious person could be so daunted by the complexity and potential for inflicting pain or creating problems that he or she might refuse to engage in life or to take any risks at all. That's where grace as well as the promise of forgiveness enter in. You'll make mistakes. It's best to acknowledge them and seek the promise of forgiveness. Grace and forgiveness enable us to jump into life, or as Thomas Merton somewhere wrote, "To forget ourselves on purpose, [and to] cast our awful solemnity to the wind and join in the general Dance." Grownups, real ones, are serious people, but they don't take themselves too seriously.

# THE PRAYER MY
# FATHER TAUGHT ME

SOMETIME BEFORE I started going to school, maybe at age four or so, my dad taught me to pray the Lord's Prayer. We said it together each night before I went to sleep. One unplanned consequence of this timing was that I developed the habit of taking a large yawn along about "Hallowed be thy name," and to this day will yawn amid the sacred words unless I have reminded myself not to. I did worry a bit about this when I became a minister. Would I yawn mid-prayer?

My family was not overtly religious. Like so many Americans of the postwar period, church was part of the middle-class American life. Being a good Christian was not that different than being a good citizen. This is to say that learning the Lord's Prayer from my father did not entail a lot of corollary religious or theological instruction, at least none that I recall. We just said it, or prayed it, and that was that. I have no idea when we stopped saying the Lord's Prayer together. I don't have any memory of doing so when I was in high school or even junior high. But I do remember the last time we said the prayer together.

Eight years before his death, my father was diagnosed with Alzheimer's disease. I'm not sure if receiving such a diagnosis is any kind of help. Generally, we like to know what our

problems are and to be able to give a name to a problem is helpful. Having a name gives us a sense, however illusory, that we
have some power over the thing that threatens us, which is,
I imagine, why we name hurricanes and tropical storms. But
when my father was diagnosed with Alzheimer's disease, there
was not a lot of hope attached to it. In fact, it probably felt to
him more like a sentence than a diagnosis. I remember him sitting at the kitchen table shortly after the session with the neu-
rologist and saying, "How have I let this happen to me?" Of
course, he hadn't *let it happen*, in the sense of being able to pre-
vent it. But like many of the questions we ask when facing bad
news, it was more a cry of lament than a question that wanted
or even expected an answer.

For the last three years of his life he was a resident in something called an "assisted living facility." He had dreaded going
to such a place, and we had dreaded it for him. It turned out
to be a good thing, both for him and for my mother, who was
until then his primary caretaker. He had always been a pretty
social guy, and frankly there was a lot more socializing in the
small assisted living facility than there was living at home and
trying to stay out of my mother's hair. Besides, it was close to
home. She could see him every day, but she didn't have to go
through the nights when he would get up and get completely
dressed at two in the morning, only to be told to get undressed
and go back to bed, and then find him up doing it all again
only half an hour later. That was probably just one of the hundreds of things to wear heavily on a caretaker for someone
with Alzheimer's.

There is sometimes humor amid this particular darkness.
Once, I decided to take the train down from Seattle, where I
live, to Eugene, where my parents lived, for a visit. My train
was scheduled to arrive in Eugene a little before midnight. I

asked my mother, well in advance, if she would hear me when I knocked on the door at that late hour. "Oh, yes, of course, I'm a very light sleeper. I'm always listening for George. Don't worry, I'll hear you." I showed up and tapped on the door. Nothing. Harder taps became loud knocks. Still nothing. Gradually, I increased the length of my knocking as well as the intensity and volume. Finally, just before I was about to break the door down, my father staggered out in his pajamas with a big, friendly smile on his face, his glasses askew. He opened the door and said, "Who are you?" I said, "I'm your son, Tony." "Oh then, come in." So I went in, went upstairs to the guest room and got into bed. Around three or so my mother suddenly sat bolt upright, thinking that I had never arrived. She clambered out of bed and began to pummel my father, saying "George, George, wake up. Tony hasn't come." By then, of course, he had no recollection of having let me in, and was completely confused by the general uproar. I guess they looked in on me and found that I was sleeping peacefully.

As his disease progressed my father spent more and more time sleeping. And after he had moved to the assisted living facility he did quite a bit of sleeping around. When I went to visit I could expect to find him on any bed in the place. He would just make himself at home and snooze away. If I woke him up he would usually be disoriented and even agitated. If, on the other hand, I simply waited until he woke up on his own he would usually be refreshed and cheerful. I learned through trial and error that the difference made it worth waiting. Alzheimer's, as I made sense of it to myself, was as if the coaxial cable made up of a hundred wires was down to about ten. If I startled my father awake the ten working lines dropped to three. But when he was rested or when the electricity was right or whatever, it was as if more lines were up and there would be stretches of something like lucidity.

One year, after I finished leading the marathon of Christmas services, I headed to Eugene for a visit. I went to his place and found him sleeping away in some bed not his own, as usual. So I waited. Sitting there, without a book to read, and realizing that I hadn't quite had my fill of Christmas carols, I began to sing. I also hoped they might penetrate his slumber with happy thoughts and associations. Often at the bedsides of the sick or elderly or those in a coma, I had found that a bit of song, especially familiar hymns, did connect to those we had otherwise given up on connecting with ever again. After three decades of three or four Christmas eve services a year, I know quite a few Christmas carols, and quite a few verses of each one. I sang them all, a couple of times, but he slept on.

So I decided I would recite some Bible passages I had committed to memory: Psalm 23, then Psalm 121, and 1 Corinthians 13. Some verses of Romans 8, plus snatches of one or two others. Then that was done. He slept on.

Since I seemed to be leading a kind of worship service (not for the first time with members of the congregation dozing off!), I decided to recite the Lord's Prayer. I knew that by heart. So I started to pray the prayer, the prayer my father taught me. As I did, his hands, which had been flat out at his sides, started to move, to rise and to float up like two huge, quivering moths, over his body. Then his hands came together and his fingers entwined. His hands were joined in prayer on his chest. I finished, "Forever and ever, amen." And at that very moment, he opened his eyes and woke up. He said, "Oh, it's you, what a nice surprise." The prayer with which he put me to sleep so many times became the prayer with which I woke him up. It was the last time we prayed it together.

# FRIENDSHIP

I N THE SCRIPTURES of the Old and New Testaments there is
ambivalence about friendship, or so it seems to me. There are
the beautiful lines of Psalm 133, which pertain not so much
to blood or family relations as they do to the bonds of friendship and unity in community: "How very good and pleasant it
is when kindred live together in unity! It is like the precious
oil on the head, running down upon the beard, on the beard of
Aaron, running down over the collar of his robes." There is also
the strange but arresting line from the book of Proverbs, "Well
meant are the wounds a friend inflicts, but profuse are the kisses
of an enemy" (Prov. 27:6). I take that to mean something like,
Better the painful honesty of a true friend than the false praise
of an enemy. The Scriptures chronicle the friendship of David
and Jonathan, among others. They even describe ancient Abraham as "God's friend." In the New Testament, as Jesus is about to
leave his disciples, he tells them, "I do not call you servants any
longer . . . but I [call] you friends" (John 15:15).

Elsewhere in the New Testament, however, Jesus seems to
criticize the partial and selective love that is friendship. Loving
your friends, those who love you, he says, is no great shakes.
"For if you love those who love you, what reward do you have?
Do not even the tax collectors do the same? And if you greet
only your brothers and sisters, what more are you doing than

others? Do not even the Gentiles do the same?" (Matt. 5:46-47). The round of friendship, of favors and greetings to and among friends, is predictable and can be self-serving. Or so it seems.

Ambivalence about friendship—appreciating its true beauty and blessings while having one's eyes open to its limits and deceptions—seems wise. I'm not suggesting that one should be suspicious of one's friends. Not at all. I am, however, suggesting that we do well to have and enjoy friends and friendships, and we do well not to limit our associations to our friends, that is, to those with whom we more or less share a lot in common and who see the world much as we ourselves do. If an impoverished life is one that has no true and fast friends, an impoverished life is *also* one that clusters too exclusively with one's friends.

To put it another, and more theological way, we human beings, at least as the Christian faith looks at us, are a strange blend of the finite and the free, of creature and creator. We are, Nathaniel Hawthorne wrote, a strange compound of "marble and mud,"[8] that is, infinite and finite. The free and creative aspect of our nature expresses itself in choosing. We choose our friends. The finite and creaturely side experiences the given nature of life. We do not choose our families, they are given. The friends we choose can relieve the burden of given relationships, whether in the intimate circle of a family or the public circle of fellow citizens. But to live too much in the realm of those we choose and not also in the realm of the given can be deceptive. It can be a flight from our finite nature and our creatureliness. The long-running television sitcom *Friends* and its imitators appeal to us precisely because they present social relationships as ours to choose. These relationships are not given, but chosen. All bonds are not really bonds. They are negotiable.

To be sure, friends and friendships are a basically good, one might say, a very good thing. But like any good thing, friendship can assume a disproportionate role or importance. My observation is that more and more, in our society, we cluster with those we choose. We hang out with people like us and with people who share our views and values. We listen to news sources and read magazines that fit our view of the world and that agree with us. Amid our freedom and choices, we feel, or so it seems to me, too little burden to come to grips with those we have been given as part of the hand we have been dealt.

During the last presidential election I read that more and more people chose their news sources, opinion columns, even online blogs less for the quality of information or reporting than simply to hear from people who think as they themselves do, to have their chosen view of the world confirmed. We talk to those who see things as we do, and of course find comfort there. But in doing so, we may end up making the world too small and flee from those relationships we have not chosen, but been given.

Let's back up a minute, however, to say more of the values of friendship. If lovers only have eyes for each other, friends tend to have their gaze turned outward together but in the same direction, toward a shared and common interest or project. Lovers stand face to face; friends stand side by side. The shared interest of friends may be fly-fishing, children, reading, political reform, building a barn, or any of a thousand other things. Friendship may endure through time and through many changing interests, or it may come to an end when a shared interest, project, or time of life is completed. It is a great joy to find those who share our passions, interests, and perspectives, those with whom we stand shoulder to shoulder in some venture, whether as small as a neighborhood block party or as large as reform of a political party or religious denomination. Having a friend at your side makes the battles bearable, the losses endurable, and the victories sweeter.

There is something wonderful about standing side by side with others in a great venture. There is something healing about going for a long walk with someone whose very presence gladdens your heart and who understands you. There is much to be said for the occasional weekend or camping trip in the company of friends. What buoys a person more, when floundering amid the high seas of life, to receive a call or note out of the blue from a friend who says, "I was just thinking about you and wondering how you are doing?" What inspires moral courage in us more than the life and example of friends who demonstrate their own moral courage? Friends and friendship are some of God's good gifts. And sometimes our very best friends are those who can say something to us that we don't want to hear, that is difficult to accept, precisely because we know that they do care for us, even love us.

Friendship is a good, but not an unqualified good. Some years ago I served a congregation that had five different services of worship. It was not because the church was overrun with people or that the sanctuary was full to overflowing. A perceptive, if somewhat sarcastic, colleague described it as "boutique worship." There were five different services for five different tastes. You choose. There was a "Big Church" service with Bach, organ, and choir. There was a chapel service, where members could discuss the sermon as they sat in the round in a small group. There was a folk music service, with guitars and tambourines. There was a family service for people with kids and music for children. And the fifth type of service had no music at all, only a discussion of whatever members felt like discussing. Many churches today have something like this, a menu of services suited to different palates. You choose the one that's right for you.

As I joined that congregation I noticed there was something else going on besides different services for different tastes. There was a rip-roaring church fight over a political issue, over which position the church would take on the issue, and over how that position would be reflected in the church's finances and investments. The conflict was real and painful, and it had the church leaders worried. My observation to the church's leaders was that it would be difficult to resolve such a conflict when members of the congregation had few opportunities for a communal experience, epitomized by the five separate options for worship services.

In some ways, this account illustrates the danger of friendship in our society at this time. We tend to gather with those who are like us, with those who we like best. It's a comfort in a crazy world to find people that share our views and values. But, in another way, it may be both more costly than we imagine and self-deceiving. We have avoided those whom we have been given, those we are stuck with. When this happens, we can't begin to understand how others—those who don't see things as we and our friends do—think or act as they do. In the congregation with the five separate services, there were five little tribes or clubs, but no real congregation. Choice had eclipsed and outweighed those whom we had been given by God through baptism.

We need friends, but we also need communities that transcend friendship and selective affinity; we need communities that comprise not those we have chosen but those who are, more or less, given to us. We need the relationships and associations we do *not* choose, those which appear increasingly in jeopardy in our society, like our family connections. Other such given relations are with those who are not our friends and need not be. They are the relationships with those we run into at the coffee shop, the farmer's market, or in the Jiffy Lube. They are our connections with the folks we encounter on the streets and in the general mix and hubbub of the public square. They are not friends. Often they are strangers, and yet they are strangers with whom we have some kind of relationship. Other such given relationships are with family, the people we do not choose, those "we are stuck with," as a friend of mine puts it.

Some years ago, shortly after I had arrived in New York City to attend seminary, I stopped on a busy street corner in New York to take in the great swirl of life: the vegetable vendors shouting their wares, the cabbies honking and swearing, people hurrying along to work, street musicians banging on instruments, and kids selling papers. As I relished it a voice whispered in my ear, "Where is God in all this?" It turned out she was a follower of the Rev. Sun Myung Moon, a "Moonie," out trolling for converts. The implication of her question was that God was nowhere to be found in all this confusion, and if I went with her, she would show me where God could be found.

I am sure that I looked wide-eyed and naïve enough to appear an excellent prospect for her message. After thinking for the briefest moment, I lifted my arms in a sort of expansive embrace of the given life before us, and with uncharacteristic extravagance declaimed, "Where is God in all this? Why God is in all of it. God is in all of this!" She immediately disappeared, having no doubt concluded that I was too far gone even for her crowd. I was, however, simply reveling in what the Quaker Parker Palmer calls "the company of strangers,"[9] the rich mix of life in the public square.

Perhaps my ambivalence about overly extolling friendship is that our lives seem increasingly privatized, defined too much to what and who we choose, and not enough engaged with those we are given. We need both: friendships we choose, and family and fellow citizens we do not. We need those with whom we share a cause and affinity, and we need those who see the world from all different points on the compass.

Martin Luther King Jr. once imagined this scenario: "A novelist died. Among his papers was a list of suggested plots, including this one, 'A widely separated family inherits a house in which they have to live together.' This is the great new problem of humanity." Learning to live together with those we have been given.

Our solution to this scenario seems to be to sell the house and divide the income, with which each will create their own little house or settlement in the midst of their friends. But King was right. We must figure out how to share the house we have all inherited and how to live with the people we are given, and not just with those we choose. The world of *Friends*, where the friends are all young, beautiful, and hip, is appealing, but it is not the real world, nor should it be.

# MARRIAGE: WHAT'S THE POINT?

MOST OF WHAT is written on the subject of marriage is in the "how-to" genre. Typical titles include *Secrets of Success in Marriage* or *The Seven Stages of a Marriage*; many books analyze the typical conflicts and points of stress of marriage, or how to attain deeper intimacy or better communication. Much of it is helpful, I'm sure, but it may also beg the larger question, which is, What's the point? Why marriage? What is the purpose of the thing? Lacking clarity or conviction about the point of marriage, we occupy ourselves with matters of technique, the how-to of sex, of communication, of money management. With some reasonably clear notion of the point of it all, many will, I suspect, manage to discover their own strategies and solutions to the challenges of marriage.

Several years ago the television writer for the *New York Times* reviewed the upcoming fall schedule of sitcoms and noted the number of shows dealing frankly and openly with relationships in their various forms. No longer were television writers and producers constrained by polite convention. They were now looking at divorce, as well as pre-, post-, and extra-marital relationships. Fair enough. There's a lot of all that. The *Times* writer concluded her review, however, by suggesting that the unasked question was, Can anyone make a case for marriage?

The implication of her more or less rhetorical question was, no one can, nor is there a case to be made. Her conclusion was that marriage has had its day. No one seems much interested in it any more. Good riddance.

In one of history's little ironies, just as the marriageable could find no real reason to want to be married (at least in the judgment of the *New York Times*), a whole new cadre of people are clamoring to be married: same-sex couples. Just when we considered marriage to be passé, irrelevant, and pointless, behold, some folks are lining up, literally, to get in on it. However, the most-often articulated reasons cited by same-sex couples for gay marriage, while not unimportant, fall far short of compelling, at least in my judgment. For some the argument for marriage is rights-based: they say people have a right to marry whomever they please. For others the primary rationale seems to be to obtain the legal and financial benefits of wedlock: eligibility for health care coverage as a spouse, access as spouse in the event of illness and hospitalization, and the retirement benefits of marriage. One can hardly disagree with any of this, but if the reason for marriage is the benefits, that can, of course, cut the other way too. Indeed, a growing number of older couples are now "shacking up" precisely because getting married has "negative tax consequences," as accountants like to put it.

What is the point of marriage? What is its purpose? The default option in our society for thinking about many things, marriage among them, is some form of cost-benefit analysis. The benefits of marriage (besides health care coverage!) are thought to be companionship, sexual intimacy, happiness, and personal fulfillment. Or perhaps marriage makes good economic sense. The problem with the cost-benefit approach is that it's not difficult to turn the thing around and call it a day. "My needs aren't being met" or "It's just not working for me" are things I have often heard from someone considering divorce. While I am not without sympathy for persons in such a situation, a cost-benefit understanding of marriage puts it on shaky ground from the beginning. That remains the case even if, at the beginning, people are ecstatic about the benefits. "I've never known anyone like her before!" "He's made me a better person!"

The purpose of marriage, so far as I can tell, is simply stated, but not easily accomplished. That purpose is the sharing of life with another person through time, or to put that slightly differently, faithfulness. Marriage begins with a promise, with giving one's word. From that point marriage is a life-long exploration of what it means to live by that promise and be faithful both to the promise and to the person to whom you have made it. For those shaped by the biblical story, faithfulness may be the key theme of that long, messy account. The biblical story is an extended meditation on the faithfulness of God to the world and to the people God has created. Marriage has long been understood within this tradition as enacting a similar faithfulness in relationship.

Of course, this faithfulness is not a mere abstract ideal. Such trust-based bonds and relationships become the basis for forming and sustaining children who have the capacity to trust others and who are themselves trustworthy. But not only the children of a marriage are affected, many others are as well. The reality of this is demonstrated in the breach. When a marriage ends in betrayal, breaking of one's promise, or divorce, the effects ripple out to touch all those who know the principals, and even many who do not know them. Of the latter, I think of the impact not only on a couple's children but on those around them in classrooms and schools. The demise of a relationship based on trust, aimed toward faithfulness, diminishes the overall trust quotient among us.

One aim, if not *the* aim, of life might well be to become persons who are trustworthy and to create human communities characterized by trust. If this is the case, then marriage is one of the crucial building blocks of such an enterprise. It is not, of course, the only crucial building block. We also want, and should want, trustworthy professions (doctors, lawyers, political leaders, and clergy) and trustworthy institutions (schools, businesses, government, hospitals, military, courts, and police). That we experience a loss of trust and broken trust in so many of these relationships and institutions is not a reason for abandoning the enterprise. It points out, rather, its value and urgency.

I have sometimes suggested to couples preparing for marriage that merely living together is the easy way. There was a time when living together was thought to be bold, unconventional, and risky while marriage was, by comparison, considered safe and conventional. It seemed to me, however, that living together without having made a clear commitment or promised oneself was much the safer of the two. Consider the marriage promise: "I (name) give myself to you (name) to be your husband. I promise to love and sustain you in the covenant of marriage from this day forward, in sickness and in health, in plenty and in want, in joy and in sorrow, so long as we both shall live." If you think about it for even a few minutes it'll knock your socks off and you'll probably want to reconsider it altogether. A lifetime is a long time. Promising to stand by someone through thick and thin, when you have no real idea of what that will entail, is not something that any self-respecting risk manager would encourage. Therein lies the point. It is a remarkably bold promise, and many would say it's a foolish promise. Therein too lies the romance. How much romance is there in telling your partner, "Let's be together so long as we're happy," which may really mean, "So long as *I'm* happy," or "Let's be together so long as you are delectable, healthy, and making money." It is perfectly understandable, but not especially bold or noble, or even romantic. The romance of a marriage commitment is the wildness of the promise and the shared venture. This extraordinary pledge to love and sustain another "till death do us part." My goodness. Is this really wise?

One recalls the scene in *Romeo and Juliet* where the young couple, who are surrounded by death and suspicion, run off to be secretly married by the priest. You get a rather vivid sense in this scene of the boldness and romance of it all. Against the odds of family feuds, violence, and revenge, Romeo and Juliet pledge themselves to one another. True, most marriages do not begin amid such inauspicious circumstances. Nevertheless, there is reason to think that Shakespeare merely makes vivid and visible the forces arrayed against faithfulness and love in this life.

The marriage promise uses the word *covenant*, which is neither much understood nor used these days. In meeting with couples prior to a wedding service, I often contrast *covenant* with *contract*. Both are binding commitments between two parties. But they are otherwise different. Contracts generally spell out with some considerable detail what each party to the contract will give and what they will get. It is certainly no accident, in these times of diminished trust, that "marriage contracts" have become popular. They represent a hedging of one's bets. Covenants, by contrast, commit us in and to a relationship not knowing precisely what that relationship will give to us or require of us. There will be both, gifts and demands, and sometimes they are all wrapped up together, as in the case of raising children. But the point of the contrast between covenant and contract is that the latter seeks to impose control over the future by specifying the conditions. A covenant, or at least the marriage covenant, advances into the unknown future on the basis of a promise, a promise to be faithful in and to this relationship—come what may.

In literature and in Scripture, covenants and life construed through the lens of covenant tend to be made of four elements. There is some sort of primal gift. In marriage it is the gift of the other person and the gift of love itself. We speak of "falling in love" in part because we sense it to be a gift not an achievement, something we have not controlled or brought about by our own devices. We have "fallen" into it. It is a gift. Or in the case of having a child, this too is experienced as a gift, the extraordinary gift of life. Oh, we may, certainly do, understand the biology of reproduction, but only the pinched soul will not at the time of birth have some sense of the miracle and the gift of it. So covenants are born of some primal gift.

The primal gift leads to some sort of promise-making moment. This is the heart and nature of a wedding service. It is all about promises and promise making. "I give myself to you to be your wife. I promise to love and sustain you in the covenant of marriage . . ." Or parents bring their children to a church or faith community for dedication or baptism. This too is the promise-making moment enacted in response to gift. Or someone graduating from a professional school (minister, doctor, or lawyer) takes the vows of her profession. It is the promise-making moment that follows on the gift of education and professional formation, which may not have always felt like a gift but remains one nonetheless. Farmers too may be aware of a covenantal relationship to the land. There is the primal gift of land and perhaps some moment of commitment and promise making as steward of the gift. This is a way of thinking about life and a way of understanding and living life.

The third element of such covenantal understanding is that life thereafter is lived and shaped by the primal gift and promissory moment. We live as those marked by gifts and promises made in response. Both the gift and the promises define identity and point to purpose. To violate either the gift or the promise is to violate ourselves. And the fourth element of covenant is the regular commemoration of the gift and promises, during which they are recalled and reenacted. At least in the case of marriage, these are expressed as anniversary celebrations, possibly renewal of marriage covenant services, or simply attending the wedding services of others, reflecting on your own, and recalling and recommitting to it. The four elements of covenant add up to shared life geared toward faithfulness, and an understanding of human beings as those who are capable of making and fulfilling promises.

I realize this may be considered, and probably is, an idealistic portrait of marriage. Moreover, based on my experience of my own marriage and on my counseling of many couples, I understand that marriage often tests and even breaks the bonds of the promises once made. This is why forgiveness is so important in marriage, and indeed in all social relationships. We need ways to heal torn relationships, to acknowledge the testing and fracture of our promises. Sometimes we need more than that. We need ways to concede that a promise cannot be fulfilled and that it is best for all involved to acknowledge its brokenness, and go our separate ways.

However, I suspect that if the footing upon which a marriage is erected is faithfulness, promise, and covenant, it will stand a better chance of being viable and life-giving than if the footing is limited to a cost-benefit calculation or the primary justification is personal fulfillment. You can pretty much count on it, or so it seems to me, that marriage will not always feel personally fulfilling.

In this way, marriage might be thought of as a discipline or a spiritual practice. It requires something like the discipline of a musician or an artist or an athlete. There may be long hours of practicing for the relatively shorter times of attainment. But without the steady practice there is no attainment. Or marriage may be analogous to a spiritual practice, for example, prayer or fasting, meditation or silence. Like any of these, I believe marriage offers the possibility of enlightenment, but not apart from the daily challenges. Some moments in a marriage are fruitful and fulfilling, and some are not. In order to experience those moments of enlightenment there will be many hours of simply keeping at it, of practicing the discipline. In the end, however, both our individual lives and our life as a people in some form of community are better when our relationships are committed and characterized by faithfulness. To increase the trust quotient is a worthy calling and a noble adventure.

# SINGING OF SEX: RE-READING THE SONG OF SONGS

S OME BIBLICAL SCHOLARS and preachers have tried to persuade us that the Bible's Song of Songs (also known as the Song of Solomon) is an elaborate allegory about the love of God for Israel or of Christ for the church. Yes, the book may have something to teach us about the divine-human relationship, but it is also, and without doubt, a song of and about erotic love. It is sensual, playful, beautiful, and filled with longing. It is an expression of joy in the pleasures of the flesh, and it revels in the beauties of the human body. The Song mostly speaks in a woman's voice—in it a woman expresses forthrightly her erotic longings.

In speaking so joyously of sexuality and in adopting a woman's voice, the Song of Songs offers a remarkable and welcome minority report within the Scriptures. The scholar Renita Weems points this out in her *New Interpreter's Bible* commentary:

> *Female sexuality [in the Bible] poses problems for men, and according to our male narrators, for God. Unrestricted contact with women threatens boundaries and portends turmoil. Repeatedly fathers warn sons against falling into the sexual snares of loose*

*women; and in both canonical and non-canonical literature one finds male narrators openly declaring their contempt for women.*[10]

The Song of Songs provides a different voice and another perspective within the Bible. Its poetry is so sensual that we can almost taste the figs and almonds and smell the fragrant oils. Its beauty is so palpable that we are prompted to weep for the ways we have misused our sexuality or missed its gift.

The Song of Songs not only contests a sexually repressive or Victorian sensibility. It also opposes the inclination toward casual sex or instant gratification that characterizes our sex-saturated society. While the Song insists that we are embodied beings and that the human body is beautiful, it also asserts that we are more than bodies.

Recently I heard someone use the phrase *the McDonaldization of sex.* What was meant by that phrase, I think, is that sex, like so much else, has come to be seen as accessible, convenient, and immediate. Why wait? "You deserve a break today!" McDonald's tells us. "Just do it!" says Nike. Fast food; fast sex.

By contrast, the Song of Songs is charged with longing. The lover seeks her beloved but does not find him. When he appears it is through a lattice or behind a fence, and their moments together are stolen.

In one respect, this feature of the Song simply reflects the society from which it emerged—a society in which relations between unmarried men and women were strictly supervised, and opportunities to be alone with a lover were few. But the language of longing and losing, of seeking and finding, expresses something more than a different cultural context. It suggests that human beings contain depths, and that love is less about knowing another's body than about learning to know another's heart. Such learning takes time and effort, and it is inevitably accompanied by frustration as well as satisfaction, sorrow as often as joy.

Several years ago the moviemaking team of Merchant and Ivory turned some of Jane Austen's novels into movies. Somewhat like the Song of Songs, these films portray love and relationships in ways that have begun to seem odd in our culture. The stories include longing and losing, seeking and finding, and are filled with small gestures that are often indirect and are sometimes missed or misinterpreted by the lovers. This is because the characters are coming to know one another's hearts slowly and carefully before they come to know one another's bodies.

The astonishing success of these films suggests that they touched a nerve in our culture and tapped into a hunger—a hunger for the acknowledgment that human beings are mysterious, that we are creatures who are not all exposed surfaces but have hidden depths, and that coming to know these depths takes time and effort. In the Scriptures of the Old and New Testaments, sexual intimacy is characteristically described as "knowing" another. Thus, Abraham came to "know" Sarah. Joseph found Mary to be great with child though he had "known her not." The term may simply be a polite euphemism, but it also suggests what we most long for and most need: to know another truly and deeply and to be known by another in the same way. This is the higher reward that comes with the higher burden imposed by older patterns of courtship and marriage.

What a difference it would make if the Song of Songs were among the books on sex that parents gave their adolescents to read. It is a book that our mother the church has given us, and that God, who loves us like a wise father, has given us. We should read it!

# SOCIAL MEDICINE: FORBEARANCE AND FORGIVENESS

T O BE SOCIAL," wrote Robert Frost, "is to be forgiving." There is some reason to think that Frost was not terribly successful at either one, being social or being forgiving. Nevertheless, his point stands, forgiveness is necessary to life in relationship with others. C. S. Lewis made a similar point, coming at it from the other end. In his book *The Great Divorce*, Lewis depicts hell as a vast, grey city inhabited only at its outer edges. There are rows and rows of empty houses in the middle because everyone who had once lived in them has quarreled with the neighbors and then moved out. Then they've quarreled with the new neighbors and moved again. That this bears some resemblance to the patterns of American cities and social mobility is disconcerting.

Forgiveness and forbearance are medicines and remedies for our social soul and relationships. Most of this essay will be focused on forgiveness, but before turning there I want to spend a little time on *forbearance*, an antique-sounding word but one I very much like. *Forbearance* seems a smaller dose of this social medicine or a preliminary stage of forgiveness. *Forgiveness* implies actual and specific wrongs done and ones that have the consequence of broken relationships. *Forbearance* suggests lesser matters, the little things that someone does or says that do not merit or require a full address, which may be best addressed by not addressing them.

To *forbear* means to "bear with" another or others. It means to endure certain minor injustices and petty grievances as well as irritating idiosyncrasies, and to refrain from response. Forbearance can, of course, be overdone and misapplied. We can forbear when we should be direct and honest and bring up a problem. But mostly we seem to live in a time when people have learned, perhaps all too well, the arts of assertiveness and complaint. We have been schooled to insist upon our due and our rights, and we are quick to make known our grievances. Thus we seem not much inclined to practice forbearance or to bear with one another in our foibles and foolishness.

The roots of forbearance, like forgiveness, lay in our own awareness of how others, or even God, have been forbearing towards us. If we are honest with ourselves, we have some awareness that each of us too has been a schmuck and a pain to get along with, and many others have had to put up with us. I have a friend, also a clergyman, who once said to me, "You know in every church I've served I've had people who would have preferred to see me six feet under." Then he smiled mischievously and added, "And you know, they had a point!" Most of us, nay all of us, are mixed bags, but, as Jesus says, God "makes the sun rise on the evil and on the good, and sends rain on the righteous and on the unrighteous" (Matt. 5:45). God forbears and endures us, and it is good that we forbear one another.

Sometimes forbearance runs out and someone takes us to task for our particular forms of self-absorption and insensitivity, but usually not until they have endured them for a good while. Moreover, what separates the wise from the foolish is not that the wise ones have never required rebuke while the foolish have. Rather, the wise are those who have the good sense to listen to a needed rebuke and to heed it, while the foolish do not listen or heed and remain clueless.

There is another aspect to forbearance that seems especially important for parents, political leaders, professionals of various sorts, as well as those in almost every leadership role or position. At least in part, forbearance means being patient in the face of provocation, or we might say, "not getting hooked." As a pastor, it took me some time and some struggle to learn this. There are times when the best response is no response, or at least not taking offense when a harsh word is directed your way. Often you can brush aside a provocation with a noncommittal response like "Thank you, let me think about that," or with humor, or with a sweet dismissal: "Oh Mary, you probably don't really mean that, do you?" It is difficult to practice forbearance when people say malicious things to you or practice deceit and manipulation. It is a kind of spiritual discipline that most effective leaders need to master, in good part because such barbs and arrows are often attempts to push a leader or group off course. If they hook you and elicit an equally harsh response, you've lost.

In families there is usually much to forbear and much opportunity to practice forbearance. In family life, we see each other much more fully, in our good and our not-so-good moments. That is both the blessing and also the curse of it. At home we can let down, and at home we do let down. Most of us have ways of doing and being that will rub others the wrong way, if not all the time then occasionally. Someone talks too much or chews too noisily or forgets to flush. Sometimes the things that bug us about others are the very same things we love about them. "He's so exuberant!" But on another day that can turn into "Do you have to be so loud all the time?" Sometimes such things can be pointed out, but if we are to live and work with others we must learn to forbear and bear with one another. It's easier if we can remember and can remind ourselves that others are also forbearing us and our little, and not-so-little, weirdnesses.

There's a Buddhist story about two monks who sat beside a river. A woman came along who needed to get to the other side. She approached the monks to ask them to carry her across. Because it was forbidden for monks to touch a woman, one of the monks declined even to acknowledge the woman's presence. But the other monk agreed to carry the woman to the far bank. He lifted her up and carried her across. Then he came back and sat down again beside his fellow monk. Six hours went by. The monk who had declined to help the woman turned to the other and asked, "Was she heavy or light?" The first monk answered him, "You are still carrying her." The strange thing about forbearance is that what we bear and carry of others we often do forget. The largeness of heart of the forbearing seems, paradoxically, to mean that they soon cease to carry the demands and slights of others that they have borne, while those less able or given to forbearance continue to be burdened by what they have refused to bear.

If forbearance in relationships is something like oil is to engines, keeping the thing moving reasonably smoothly and reducing friction, then forgiveness is more on the order of anything from a tune-up to a complete engine overhaul. I put it this way because we too often confuse forgiveness with forbearance, and believe that an oil change will do when a tune-up or major overhaul is required. Forgiveness is not just bearing with or enduring. Nor is forgiveness a solo act, it involves interaction and, yes, confrontation. Nor is forgiveness merely a sentiment or a feeling; it is a practice, something we do. Forgiveness is real work, and often tough work, and it is costly too. This is not a ten-minute oil change.

Moreover, we cheapen and misunderstand forgiveness when we reduce it to "letting bygones be bygones" without ever having done the work to name the problems or the brokenness. We trivialize forgiveness when we shrug and tell ourselves to forgive and forget, and allow that to excuse us from facing the matter and the person involved. These may be aspects of forbearance, of enduring and bearing with one another, of cutting one another some slack. But they are hardly the right response when the engine, or the relationship, is broken or when the four or six cylinders of a relationship have been reduced to two cylinders. When that's happened, you can add all the oil you want, but it quickly burns up and spews forth foul fumes into everyone's air.

Forgiveness is required when a relationship has been broken or damaged, which leads to an important point and distinction. Forgiveness may well entail absolving guilt, but that is not the primary point or purpose of forgiveness. Forgiveness is about restoring a relationship. This is important to keep in mind. When it is forgiveness that you are practicing and restored relationship that you seek, then naming the break and the hurt is important, but you don't do it to hurt the other back or exact a sort of revenge, but because you want to regain and restore that relationship. Before joining a confrontation, it makes a big difference if we know what our goal is and what we are hoping to achieve. When it is forgiveness we are working at, the goal and purpose is to restore the relationship, to win back something that has been lost, to heal or mend something that has been broken. That's the first element of the practice of forgiveness: The goal is to get the relationship back and in working order.

I remember the first time I asked one of my sons to forgive me. I do not now remember what I had done or said that needed forgiveness. I expect I had spoken too sharply to him, or had spoken in anger and scared him badly. Whatever it was, I knew immediately that I had broken something between us. I could, and probably did, offer excuses and rationalizations: "stress at work," "too tired," "he shouldn't have said . . ." But the point was that I had been out of line, had been too sharp or unfair or angry. It's a humbling thing for a parent to ask forgiveness from their child. Mine was probably ten or twelve at the time. But I did ask for it, acknowledging that I had been wrong, that I shouldn't have said what I did or do what I had done. He forgave me, and our broken relationship was, figuratively, at least splinted and set for healing.

Here's a second element of the practice of forgiveness. The person who has been hurt or offended may need to take the initiative in the practice of forgiveness. In teaching about forgiveness Jesus recommends this surprising strategy, that the person who has been hurt or offended be the one to initiate the process of forgiveness. This may seem odd, even wrong or unfair. "She is at fault, so let her come to me," we think. "I didn't do anything wrong; he's the one who needs to apologize."

By asking the offended party to get the ball rolling, Jesus may be aware of two possibilities. Sometimes the offending party may be clueless and not aware that they have done something that has hurt you and jeopardized, if not broken, your relationship. The offender may not even know they have screwed up. I have been in that spot. Someone comes to me to say that what I said or did has deeply hurt them, and I didn't even know it. If they hadn't brought it up, it never would have come up, and the relationship would have been permanently damaged, and I wouldn't have had a clue about why or been given the opportunity to put it right again.

Jesus may have had something else in mind by suggesting that the offended party take the initiative: a person in that position must fight against seeing themselves as a victim. Jesus understood that sometimes we cannot avoid being victims, but we *do* have a choice about adopting a victim mentality, one where we get stuck savoring our hurts instead of salving them with a healing balm, or one where we cede our power to the other person or party. This is what is at stake in Jesus' famous recommendations to "turn the other cheek" and "walk the second mile." The idea is not to be a doormat, but to take control and use your power. Turn the other cheek. Walk a second mile. Up the ante. By taking the bull by the horns, with the offended going to the offender and initiating a resolution, the victim claims and exercises power and avoids the trap of the victim mentality, which may in the end prove even more damaging than being a victim.

Implied in both of these elements of the practice of forgiveness—the goal to restore a relationship and the need for the offended party to initiate the process—is a third element: the process of forgiveness involves confrontation. *Confrontation* probably sounds like something bad, but it doesn't have to be. It literally means coming "face to face" with the problem and with the person with whom we have a problem. If often we actually undermine or misunderstand the nature and process of forgiveness with formulas or slogans like "forgive and forget," the better alternative may be to "remember and forgive."

On the larger societal scale, we have witnessed this process of forgiveness several times in recent years, most notably in South Africa with its Truth and Reconciliation Commission in the wake of the apartheid era. The guiding assumption of the commission was that forgiveness becomes possible only when evil and the injustice are remembered and named. Victims were not asked to forget but to remember, to remember and to tell their story. Only then are victims in a position to forgive. In our personal relationships, we may not require something so grand as a commission for truth and reconciliation, but the remembering and naming of grievances is important, even crucial, to the process of forgiveness.

It used to puzzle me that in virtually every Easter story, every story of an appearance to the disciples of the risen and resurrected Jesus, he visibly bears the wounds of crucifixion. He never appears, in any of these stories, without spot, wound, or blemish. On the contrary, in all these instances he bears the scars of the ordeal. There is mention of the nail holes in his hands or the wound where the spear penetrated his side. Is this just about blood and gore, I wondered? Yuck. Then it made sense. There is no sanitizing, no whitewashing, no cover-up. There's no pretending it didn't happen. The wounds are real. The suffering is real. The betrayal is real. The death is real.

Often in families and churches and a thousand other places we try to have a resurrection without ever acknowledging that there has been a crucifixion. We say, in effect, OK, let's all be nice and happy and get along, even while you're thinking, Wait a minute, there's dead and wounded people all over the place! When the pain and brokenness and wrongs are faced and acknowledged, then forgiveness also becomes a real possibility. It is not "forgive and forget," but "remember and forgive."

Of course, there are situations where the offending party refuses to acknowledge any problem or responsibility for an offense. In such a situation Jesus counsels a tough thing, something that many might even consider to be un-Christian. He says that we should treat such a person as a Gentile or a tax collector, in other words, as someone who is outside the community. That may sound awful, but it strikes me as even more awful to pretend that you haven't lost a relationship when you have, to pretend that you can go on as if nothing's happened when you can't. Jesus didn't ask his followers to pretend. There are some people who are unwilling or unable to own any responsibility on their part for the brokenness of things. It is always someone else's fault. Psychologists may call it a narcissistic personality disorder or some form of sociopathic behavior. It may be a good idea, and the best you can do, to simply give such a person a wide berth and try to otherwise practice damage control.

Like forbearance, extending forgiveness to others becomes a possibility when we have been on the receiving end of forgiveness ourselves. Thus, Jesus said, "Forgive one another, as God has forgiven you." Of course, if you think of yourself as without fault or as someone not needing forgiveness, then you have a different kind of problem, which either is that you are a numbskull or self-deceived or self-absorbed or all three. Some get over this simply by living beyond the age of thirty, for others it may require a more serious wake-up call. But the point is that before forgiveness is a task, something for us to do, it is a gift, something done for us. If we are stuck in the process and practice of forgiveness and can't seem to entertain the possibility of extending forgiveness to another, it may help to spend some time reflecting on when and how and what you have been forgiven.

When I was a young man I found it difficult to acknowledge mistakes or to say "I'm sorry." But as time went by, and in such a visible and complex role as that of a pastor, I learned that mistakes, rather than being the end of the world, are very much a part of the world and inevitable. Moreover, I found that saying "I'm sorry" (and meaning it) is not a cause for shame or terminal mortification, but an occasion for learning and growing. As some have observed, Christians are not perfect, just forgiven. Or a phrase I like even better, the final work of grace is to make us gracious. (For more, see the essay "On Grace.")

Families and churches, even nations, can either be schools of forbearance, forgiveness, and reconciliation, or they can be schools of silence and pretense, and of a pretend harmony. Meanwhile, old grudges fester and live on. They are even treated like closely held and carefully managed assets. Which skills are we teaching in our families and our communities? Are we extending the ugly sprawl as people move farther and farther out, or are we involved in a great movement of urban renewal, back to the neglected and abandoned centers of town, there to renew life and relationships?

# WHAT ARE
# FATHERS FOR?

WHAT ARE FATHERS for? Are fathers indispensable or dispensable? What is it exactly that fathers do, or that they are supposed to do? Like so many things, these questions are prompted by social changes that are both positive and negative. On the plus side, gender roles are less restrictive or prescribed than was the case a generation or two ago. It is not so clear as it once was, that women do this and men do that. The negative side of things is that too many fathers are simply missing in action. Perhaps they never married the woman who gave birth to their child or children, and have then disappeared altogether. Or maybe they have only a minor role as a result of divorce or custody battles. For too many children, life is *Life Without Father*, the title of a recent book that studied and enumerated the negative consequences of such a development.

When we were expecting our first child, we lived in Hilo, Hawaii, a small town on the windward side of the island of Hawaii, also known as "The Big Island." Across the street lived Miss Katherine Beveridge, a regal yet warm and lively octogenarian. Katherine's father had captained whaling ships, and she came to Hawaii aboard one around the turn of the century. She had lived her entire life there in Hilo, teaching elementary school. Though she had never had children of her own, she had taught hundreds of children all over the island and knew as much about kids and parents as anyone I've ever known. By the time we got to know her, Katherine was at that stage of life where she was shrinking in size but still large, even growing, in stature.

As my wife's pregnancy advanced I must have felt some anxiety about fatherhood because one day I wondered aloud to Katherine about how I would do as a parent and as a father. She laughed a bit and said, "You'll do fine, just trust yourself." She saw that what I needed was less a matter of instruction and more a dose of reassurance. There is no real or adequate instruction for the business of being a father. It's too big, too variable, and too open-ended. But for all those reasons we do need reassurance and we need trust.

What do fathers do? Are fathers providers, disciplinarians, supporters, teachers, guides, lawgivers, defenders, coaches, or confidants—all of the above or none of the above? I think I have played all those roles for my own children, two sons and a daughter, though with varying degrees of success. Nevertheless, I am not sure any one of the list, nor the entire list taken together, answers the question "What are fathers for?" The real answer seems so obvious as to be hidden in plain sight. Fathers are part of the primal human community that engages in the most basic and most complex of tasks: raising the next generation. The oft-cited proverb "It takes a whole village to raise a child" starts with the very first village of two different people. It is probably no accident that this proverb became popular about the time life without father was becoming much more common.

If it is true that parents must strive for a balance between two kinds of love—accepting love and transforming love— then a father and a mother may embody these two kinds of love and in doing so balance one another. If accepting love affirms the being of a child and lets them be, then transforming love seeks their well-being and prods their growth. The interesting and probably controversial question is if a father's (or a mother's) love is necessarily one of these two loves? In other words, does a mother's love tend to be the accepting love, while the father's love is the transformative complement, or vice versa? And if each kind of love can be assigned to one parent, is that nature's proper order or society's preferred construction? Surely, the two loves can and do dwell in one person. Surely, too, there are countless incidences when the father's love is more of the accepting variety and the mother's love more of the transforming.

These are questions to which I have no answer. What I do have, however, is this observation: it is the father's blessing that is more often than not the one that is sought and in some sense earned as opposed to given freely. If true, this suggests that more often it is the father who holds or conveys the transforming love. In my own life, and in many others, I have heard stories of the father's blessing being given; not nearly so often, rarely in fact, have I heard similar stories of the giving of the mother's blessing. This may be because of the nature of childbirth and nurture. Mothers and children are bound together at the beginning while fathers are at an inevitable distance. Or it may be because, whether by nature or nurture, fathers tend to more often be the embodiment of the transforming love while mothers embody an accepting love.

I certainly remember how long I waited before receiving a blessing from my own father, who had Alzheimer's disease. During his last three years he lived in a small facility with twenty others in various stages of the disease. Often I visited him alone, simply because it was harder for my wife to get away from work. However, the summer before he died we were both there for a visit. The three of us were walking together arm in arm, my wife and I on either side of him. We moved at his slow place across the dining room toward the door, which led to an enclosed garden. By this time my dad seldom said much that made sense to us. Even his words had become difficult to understand, his speech often slurred. As we crossed the dining room his slippered shuffle drew to a halt. Bent over, he looked up at me and clear as a bell said, "You are a good man." Then he resumed his shuffle toward the door. My wife said, "Did you hear that?" She did not mean, "Did you hear the words he said?" She meant, "Did you hear, really hear, what he was saying to you?" It was my father's blessing. Three months later he died.

Even though I have heard such stories of a father's blessing many times as a pastor, my own experience of it came as if I had never heard a one. It was as unexpected and as pleasing a gift as a rainbow. But almost all the stories of such blessings seem to be stories of the father's, not the mother's, blessing. The mother's blessing seems to have been imparted long ago, at the womb, and requires no conferral. Yes, clearly there are many exceptions to this as a pattern, but the pattern itself stands. In this sense, it is the father's love that is more of the growth-prodding and demanding, while a mother's is more of the accepting and letting be.

But this exploration of the double face of love, or the two loves of parents, can be taken a step further. So often in life truth lies in holding the tension of competing truths, in holding "the tension of polarity," as Kierkegaard put it. The tension between accepting love and transforming love should never be resolved in favor of one pole or the other. Both poles are absolutely necessary. One does not solve or resolve such polarities, one lives with them, balancing and managing them. Having two parents is like having both ends of the seesaw occupied.

This can be tough. I say, "time to let go," while my wife says, "time to hold on." Usually we're both right and both are true. Wisdom lies in finding the course between. Being a father is being part of this duo and duet, this dance, and holding down your side of the seesaw of things. Left to our own devices and desires, many of us would tilt out of balance. My hat is off to those who manage the daunting job of raising kids as single parents, but I don't envy them. Two parents in it together is a good idea whenever possible. We all need other people who are close enough to the situation and close enough to us to give us an honest reality check, to keep us balanced even as we balance the other.

The trick in all the various roles parents play is doing it without overdoing it. The Taoist philosopher Lao-tzu once counseled the emperor "to govern as you would fry a small fish—lightly." Children are small fish, and at least for a time, parents loom as large as emperors. Our touch as parents and as fathers needs to be light but firm; doing enough but not overdoing it. Providing but not providing everything, protecting without hovering, nurturing without stifling, teaching without being heavy-handed.

Because so much of being parents seems to be about doing but not overdoing, I return to the obvious but lately problematic point about what fathers are for. Being a parent is not a solo act. Neither fathers nor mothers have a child, so far, by themselves. The seesaw nature of parenthood is good reason for two parents to be involved and engaged, balancing one another and thus raising reasonably balanced children. What are fathers for? The answer is hidden in plain sight. We are an essential part of the parental package, part of the first and primary human community our children know.

# DEATH DIMINISHED

I N A SECTION of essays on relationships, death may seem an intruder. Does not death signal the end of relationships? Relationships seem not only the stuff of life but a good part of what makes life worth living. What's death doing here? Of course that is the question death always presses upon us: What are you doing here? What do we make of death?

One of the blessings of the ministry is that you spend a fair amount of time dealing with death. In contrast to most people, for whom death remains a relative stranger, for a pastor death is a regular visitor and acquaintance. A pastor visits the dying in their final days and hours. Sometimes a pastor is present at the moment breathing ceases, a moment as mysterious as birth. I often have sat with those who feel the sting of a particular death most acutely. I am given the task of articulating the faith of a community at the time of death. But it doesn't end there. As the years go by, the dead and departed continue as a presence. This is built into the life of the church with its periodic remembrances of the saints—"we also are compassed about with so great a cloud of witnesses," as Paul puts it in Hebrews 12:1 (KJV). Beyond that, I have found that the dead of your congregation do live on in your awareness. I hesitate to use the word *ghost* because of its many occult connotations. Still, it feels something like that. I remember someone who lived in that apartment, who loved that book, who had that funny way of nodding his head or had that great smile, or who called on election day to trumpet the results. As we get older, we all have memories of those who have died. Pastors may simply have known more of those who have already passed than most people.

The ways in which death is observed have changed during the years of my ministry. At my first church in a rural area in the Northwest, most services were funerals, that is, the body of the deceased was present in a casket at the front of the church. During seminary there was discussion about how to work with funeral homes and their staff, as well as the relative merits of closed and open caskets. Thirty years later, the traditional funeral has all but vanished, and teaching future pastors about it is no longer relevant. Today funerals have been replaced by memorial services, that is, services without the body present. The open (or closed) casket is largely a thing of the past.

At my first church the casket in a traditional funeral was carried or escorted at the end of the service by pallbearers to a waiting hearse. The hearse, a great black station wagon, was driven slowly along the main street of town as people either walked or drove behind. I usually walked behind the hearse, clerical robes flapping in the wind. It was a short distance to the cemetery on the other side of the elementary school. Usually the kids on the playground would press up against the fence to watch the proceedings. I am sure it all looked to them like something out of the movies. My robes blowing with the breeze as mourners, clinging to one another, stumbled to their places at the graveside. The words were said, solemn and ancient, then the casket was lowered into the ground. Afterwards, the mourners went someplace, often back to the church, to eat something together and talk, signs that life goes on.

Today, less than thirty years later, things are remarkably different. Memorial services have replaced funerals, cremation has replaced burial, and ashes are interred or scattered in a great variety of places. The caveat to these generalizations is to note that there are great variations in all this according to region and culture. Probably what I've described is more the case in the more secular and mobile west, and less true in other parts of the country that remain more traditional. But what do these changes in what we do at the time of death mean?

Generally speaking, death and the rituals surrounding death have become less public in nature and more personal and private. The pallbearers, hearse, procession through town, public burial with schoolchildren looking on through the fence, all are aspects of a public occasion and ritual. It was visible in the figurative public square, according to inherited custom or tradition, and it interrupted, halted for a time, the round of daily life. I can imagine that for an elementary school student this spectacle would have been both arresting and thought-provoking. I can also easily imagine an earnest parent these days petitioning the principal or school board to put up a fence or concrete wall to avoid upsetting the children.

Today death and its attendant rituals seem a great deal more private than they once were. Rather than calling a halt to business as usual, the memorial service can be scheduled whenever it is convenient since there's no body in a casket to worry about. While some services at the time of death proceed according to inherited ritual and practice, there tends to be a great deal more innovation, customizing, and personalizing. People invent new rituals or appropriate ones they have seen elsewhere and liked. Moreover, there's more emphasis on the person of the deceased. Frequently stories of the deceased are recounted, memories shared, and mementos exhibited. Often today there is no public site or visible designation, like a tomb-stone, of the location of the final remains. They are scattered into the sea, a river, on a mountainside, or in a backyard. The immediate family may know the place, but for others there is no sign or indication.

What are we to make of these changes? Are they good or bad, or some of both? The greater focus on the person who has died can certainly be positive. It gives a service a kind of real-ity and personal quality that isn't found when simply marching through a liturgy that's exactly the same for whomever has died. But there's something else to consider. Not only can such recollections and tributes simply go on too long or become maudlin, but after the death of a loved one their survivors often crave a larger sense of meaning, a framework of belief; and if the survivors are a part of a faith community, they may want a perspective on the transcendent source of life and meaning. I wonder sometimes if the expansion of personal emphasis is an attempt to fill a vacuum once occupied by a more sturdy and widely shared faith.

The diminished public aspect of death rituals certainly makes it less an ordeal and expense. But it may be another way in which contemporary culture cloisters death to keep it from being too visible or too intrusive. While death has become more personal or personalized, with the varied celebrations of the life of the deceased, it is also, paradoxically, diminished, smaller. No great public drama is enacted, only a private ritual and moment. No town cemetery keeps the dead a visible pres-ence in our midst. Today they disappear upon wind and wave.

In recent memory, there have been times that death demanded our attention and even put a halt to business as usual. There is still some of this, but less than once was true. Memorial services have become popular, at least in part, because death can be fit to our schedules. It is not uncommon today for a pastor trying to schedule a service to be told, "No, not then, we're on our trip to Mexico" or "I am so sorry but our daughter and her family have their ski vacation that week." Death doesn't quite have the capacity it once had to interrupt our lives. Does this mean we've come to some sort of peace with death and that we accept it? Perhaps, but the opposite seems also a likely possibility, that is, we keep death at bay by keeping to our schedules and busy lives.

The Scriptures say that in the midst of life, we are in death. Death is ever present and a part of life. Death is always near. The altered and diminished public rituals attending death seem, on balance, to be our attempt to forget or conceal this truth. While it is clear that anyone who broods constantly on the topic of death has a problem, it is also true that the denial of death is among the deepest and most powerful of our self-deceptions. Moreover, it deprives us of death's salutary possibilities, which include reminding us of the preciousness and urgency of life.

In one of the Bible's frankest and most majestic meditations on human finitude, there is the following verse: "Teach us to number our days aright, that we gain a heart of wisdom" (Ps. 90:12, NIV). The point is clear. We shall not live forever. We have limited time to act, to forgive, to make peace, to savor beauty, to do the things that only we can do, to love. We don't have forever. And if that were not enough, we don't have any real clue about when death may come. Oh, we can consult the actuarial tables on life expectancy and so on, but they trade in generalities, not our specific life. Just as imminent death can sometimes deepen and transform a person, so an awareness of death in the midst of life can increase perspective, heighten humility, and generally help us to take seriously matters that are truly serious while letting go of those that are not so serious. All of this is to say that death and our sober awareness of it has ethical meaning and consequence. It can make us wise and good.

Alexander the Great had among his retinue of servants one whose responsibility was to say daily to Alexander, "My Lord, you too shall die." These days most of us in the first world have some measure of the power and protection against life's vicissitudes, if not the fame, of an Alexander. We can kid ourselves into thinking we shall live forever, and indeed some are working pretty hard at making it a possibility. Perhaps we need something like Alexander's servant who punctures our denial to say, "You too shall die."

Death does not only have the possibility of imparting ethical meaning and a sense of urgency to life, it puts us in touch with mystery, with the possibility of transcendence. Often enough I have left a home where death has occurred and felt an odd sense of gratitude, not for the death, though sometimes death's arrival is welcome, but gratitude for the gift of life. Death reminds us that life is both mystery and gift, not something we can control, but only something we can receive with gratitude.

Recently we gathered as a family for Thanksgiving dinner. In my prayer before we ate I gave thanks for, among other things, time made precious by its passing. About three-quarters of the way through dinner, my father-in-law, who is ninety-two, began to act a bit strange. Suddenly his speech was slurred and his answers incoherent. His eyes had glazed over and his right hand trembled. He seemed near to passing out. Of course, we all jumped up, started taking his pulse, and peppered him with questions: "What's your name? Do you know what day it is?" One of us called 911. An ambulance and emergency medical technicians came and gave him oxygen.

He went to the hospital for observation. He turned out to be OK, just momentarily overcome. Later, we attributed it to a particularly long-winded uncle who had, it seems, finally succeeded in talking someone straight into a coma!

But the dinner was changed. We had been sobered by the remembrance that in the midst of life we are in death. Everything seemed more precious, and life itself a miracle. Our Thanksgiving had not been ruined, it had been deepened and made real.

PART THREE

# ON SOCIETY

# NOTES OF A FIELD-BASED SCHOLAR: A VIEW OF MINISTRY

URING MY SECOND, "middler" year at New York's Union Theological Seminary, my family and I headed to upstate New York as part of a new field-based studies program. I was to serve as student pastor of a small, rural congregation while taking part in the continuing education programs of area ministers, many of whom were themselves recent graduates of Union Seminary. It was here that I was introduced to the idea of a pastor as a field-based scholar by men and women who were living it. Several of those pastors also had academic doctoral degrees, and yet they were content—more than content, excited—to lead congregations, even small, rural ones. They spoke of the historic self-understanding of rabbis as field- and community-based scholars and teachers, an idea I loved immediately and latched onto. I had found my calling and I had found my people!

Such a notion of the minister as a field-based scholar might be thought romantic. But as Alfred North Whitehead observed, romance is the necessary first step in the dance of learning. Without romance you never get on the dance floor. You have to fall in love with something to learn it. The next step in Whitehead's educational three-step, discipline, is learning how to stay on the dance floor beyond your initial infatuation. It means learning the craft when you're tired and the work becomes too demanding or monotonous. Whitehead's third step, which he called generalization, is becoming proficient enough at your work to make wider applications, to generalize from that experience to other situations. The rabbinical idea of a community-based scholar was pure romance to me and got me out on the dance floor for good.

Many clergy today claim they are far too busy for study, for engaging ideas and texts, or for writing or interpreting an intellectual and moral tradition and way of life. I suppose they have a point. Ministry is relentless in its demands on a pastor, and sustained study or intellectual life can easily slip to the bottom of the list. Ministry requires much of a person in sheer energy and emotional resilience as you bounce from crisis to crisis in increasingly shaky or fragile institutions. Still, when I hear ministers say they never have time to read or aren't much interested in ideas, I wonder to myself "What do you do?" I am afraid that what too many of us do these days is try to invent or promote whatever programs or activities will attract people and keep the ship afloat. Like the other professions, such as medicine and law, ministry too has been overtaken by the market, a sad and corrupting fate.

For nearly thirty years I've thought of the ministry as the work of a field-based scholar and teacher, and have found some considerable delight in it. I was not a scholar for the guild of scholars, nor did I wish to be. I was a scholar for a diverse community of ordinary people, for those who worked as farmers and lawyers, schoolteachers and military officers, housewives and students. I was steeped in the world of ideas, and I was also up to my waist, sometimes over my head, in the thick of the lives of people and families, congregations and cities, and their trials and triumphs. It was perfect for me. It's a good life.

As a minister I felt I had the opportunity and the responsibility to think, speak, write, and act from the faith and tradition I represented. Of course, that meant I needed to know and understand the tradition, which too few clergy actually do. It meant interpreting the tradition, sometimes challenging it, but more often being challenged by it. I tried to speak and write from my faith tradition, particularly when I spoke in the wider community. That is, I did not want to speak as some sort of generic moral or community leader. I tried to speak as a Christian. In so doing I hoped to invite others to speak from their context and tradition, whether Jewish or Islamic, Buddhist or another spiritual or ethical perspective. I did not feel a need to prevail over other faiths or perspectives. I was eager to be enriched by them and engage in a dialogue. I thought we might each remind and call one another to be the best of our respective traditions and faiths.

This was not always easy, particularly and ironically for those who understood themselves as liberal or as modern. For such as these, and in many ways I am one, there tends to be a suspicion of tradition and an infatuation with the new. The things that are new, latest, improved are usually presumed to be better, an assumption that seems, to me at least, open to question. Nevertheless, this often led more liberal clergy and their followers to pick and choose from many and varied traditions, and to incorporate whatever was the latest fad or fashion. I didn't find this particularly appealing. Worse, it seemed to lack integrity.

I was eager to go deep into one faith and tradition, but it needed to be a tradition that was, in the words of the art historian Jaroslav Pelikan, a "living tradition." Pelikan distinguished *tradition* from *traditionalism.* "Tradition is the living faith of the dead; traditionalism is the dead faith of the living."[1] It was tradition as a living faith that I sought and, I must say, found in Christianity. To be sure, there are many Christians who seem attached to the dead faith of the living, but that ought not obscure a terrifically rich and varied living tradition.

Part of the tradition (small "t") of the Protestant Reformed strand of Christianity draws from John Calvin and other reformers the conviction that all of life is lived before and unto God. This is a corollary of biblical monotheism and is really profoundly Jewish. It means that human beings cannot divide up their lives into separate compartments, into family life, a job or economic life, a political life, and then a spiritual life. It means that religion is not just for Sunday, after which we're something different or someone else again on Monday. It all hangs together or it doesn't hang together at all. We are a whole. All of life is lived before and unto God.

Not only does this help make life interrelated and whole, it gives a person like me license to be interested in almost anything, though I probably didn't need such permission. As a crusty old theologian once remarked, "God cares about lots of things besides religion." This Protestant conviction does seem to be in my bones, and though I love the church I grow restive when things become too spiritual, if that refers to some special spiritual realm that beckons us away from life in all its earthy and earthly glory.

The trick is to see life—all of life—through the lens and perspective of this faith, this story of God's mysterious, persistent, and surprising grace. The essays in this section evidence my attempt to contemplate the large canvas of life through that lens. There are reflections here on war, terrorism, homosexuality, pluralism, and citizenship, to name a few of our contemporary conundrums. Several of these pieces first appeared in the Focus section of the *Seattle Post-Intelligencer*, for which I write a regular opinion column. I've also spent a good deal of time thinking about and trying to practice leadership, and that is considered explicitly in one essay and implicitly in several others. I conclude with a piece that tries to make some sense of "post-modernity" and the challenges of living in the midst of the great sea change in which we find ourselves.

In an age of specialists and experts, ministers and religious leaders should embrace the role of generalists. The world needs some generalists. But a generalist is not the same as a dabbler. A generalist undertakes a variety of tasks and has many different interests, but seeks or looks for the connections and for the unity that is at the heart of things. A generalist is a person who sees the forest beyond the trees. The word *religion* can, in fact, be traced etymologically to the word from which we derive *ligament.* In a world so often fragmented into a thousand little bits and pieces, religion is about the connections, our social and spiritual ligaments, those things that connect us to each other and to the sacred. It is about finding the links and the patterns, weaving the varied threads together, and delighting in the connections that are discovered. This is the opportunity of the pastor, the field-based scholar. It's a good life.

# COMMUNITY

I WAS BORN AND raised in the era following World War II when three relatively new devices were changing the face of America: the automobile, the air conditioner, and the television. In the postwar era all were in mass production and distribution. The automobile meant that we could travel farther and more often, really whenever we felt like it, whether to work or for leisure. It also meant that our bonds to those nearest to us were weakened. We were on the road and on the go. In time, the near-universal acquisition of cars meant that cities, neighborhoods, and shopping areas took on a new look altogether. They were designed for people in cars and for people who had to park their cars. Cities and states were crisscrossed with four-lane highways, and then six- and eight-lane freeways, to let the cars get to where they needed to go. But the very highways that made cars useful and efficient sliced up cities and communities, creating asphalt divides. Often the bigger roadways were nearly impassable by pedestrians.

Air conditioners seemed a veritable godsend to residents who endured the sweltering summers in Washington, D.C., when I was a kid. We got our first one sometime in the early 1960s. Before that, summer nights in that humid climate meant tossing and turning on sweat-drenched sheets until the temperatures finally became bearable around 3:00 A.M. But air conditioning, as not a few sociologists soon observed, meant something else. People stayed inside their homes, where it was cool. They left their front porches, back stoops, and yards. They shut their doors and windows. They weren't outside, where they could visit with the neighbors or watch the kids play "kick the can" on summer evenings.

Television completed this trifecta of modern improvements. We huddled around the little black-and-white screens that gradually grew to be large, color models. But some other forms of entertainment vanished as television sets became ubiquitous. The public lecturer on tour, the dramatic monologist, and the vaudeville show—all forms of art, public speaking, and entertainment that reached large audiences—pretty much vanished. Theater, symphony, opera, and ballet survived in the larger cities, but they were always aware of the powerful competition of the television (and now the home video and entertainment center).

At just about the time these three wonders of the modern age were taking hold, Harry Emerson Fosdick, then minister of New York's Riverside Church, wrote his best-known hymn, "God of Grace and God of Glory." It contains many memorable lines, but perhaps the one most etched in my own mind describes our society as "Rich in things, but poor in soul." Fosdick's analysis was compelling, but in some ways it might have been even more accurate, if less singable, had he written "Rich in things, but poor in *community*." Each of the three—the automobile, the air conditioner, and television—struck a blow, if unintentionally, at community. Whether casual or planned, in the neighborhood or at churches, Grange Halls, and community centers, the ways people gathered changed. Changed and diminished. This is a great example of an odd way in which prosperity is not always good for community.

The converse is true too. Not only does there often seem to be more public life and community in places where people have less, but community spirit regularly blossoms when disaster strikes. I remember that during a short stint living in Cambridge, Massachusetts, we got to know our neighbors at a midnight pajama party on the street. The building fire alarm started screaming just before midnight, sending us all outside for a mixer. Seldom does disaster break upon us—whether flood, storm, or power outage—without people remarking afterwards on how the community pulled together, and even though it was tough, it was also wonderful to feel so, well, together, and part of something. We are victims of our own success. Lonely amid the appliances, we need nothing but one another.

One night at about 10:30, after we were all in bed, there was a loud banging on our front door. When I opened it I was face to face with a big guy who looked a little roughed up and worse for wear. He had gauze wrapped around his head and more gauze bandages wrapped around an arm. Urgently, he blurted out, "You know me, we live just up the street," he said, gesturing to a house a few doors away. He moved quickly on in hurried speech about an accident, a wife in the hospital, and his need for money for medicine. Alarmed by his bandages and his urgency, I asked how much he needed. And then I thought, I don't know this guy. I know everyone who lives down the street and he doesn't live here. "You know," I said, "I don't think I know you; what did you say your name was?" "Jack." "And where do you live, Jack, at what address?" "Well, you know, just down the street." It was a scam, the police said later. This guy was knocking on doors, looking like he'd been beat up, telling people he was a neighbor, and asking for money. They said this scam had been showing up in recent weeks in our part of town. It was a scam predicated on the con artist's confidence that we didn't know our neighbors. And there was a good chance his gamble would have paid off, except that the neighborhood had recently had a block party and potluck at the end of our cul-de-sac.

It is easy to put a dollar value on televisions, cars, air conditioners, and all the other stuff with which we furnish our lives. These things and their various technological descendents are part of growing economy and of the good life. It's harder to put a dollar value on community. But make no mistake, it is valuable. There is value, in ways we can't easily quantify like on a bank statement, when we know and are known by our neighbors. It is worth a lot when you have people with whom you share the chapters and changes of life, and care together about schools. It means everything not to be alone when alone doesn't mean solitude but loneliness.

So community in recent days has become something we work at, seek, build, and choose to participate in (or not). This changes what community means. There was a time when communities, like families, were not so much the people you choose as they were the people you were stuck with. There were some you liked, and some you loved. There were some you found irritating and some that pretty well drove you crazy. But you were in it together.

These days our communities come to resemble affinity groups, people gathered around a common interest or people who are more or less similar. Such communities offer company to their members, and sometimes a great deal more. But there's something a little artificial about them too. There's so little real life—political, economic, or geographical—that binds the people together in many of our contemporary versions of community.

Perhaps aware of the way that the decline of earlier forms of community has led to affinity groups in their place, a friend of mine once made the tart comment that "Community is where the person you least want to be with always is; and should he or she leave, someone (pretty much like them) takes their place." It's true, community is not made up of only pleasant people, our friends, or people who bright, happy, healthy, and good-looking. Community that is worthy of the name is always a mixed bag. In community we learn patience in bearing with others. In the course of it we become aware of something else—that others have been patient in putting up with us.

# THE PROBLEM
# OF PLURALISM

THE BENEFITS OF being a pluralistic society or community, one that is made up of many different and distinct parts and perspectives, are often celebrated as diversity or multiculturalism. Such pluralism offers a diversity of viewpoints and experiences as well as a greater number of voices at the tables of discussion and decision. Varied constituencies organize to express and articulate their needs. The table is enlarged. These are genuine and significant benefits. What is not so often noted, and still less addressed, is the problem of pluralism. John Gardner, the founder of the citizen's lobby Common Cause, put that this way: "The problem of pluralism is the war of the parts against the whole."[2]

I recalled Gardner's insight as I observed our school board's recent, and unsuccessful, search for a new school superintendent. Four finalists were invited to the city. All four were examined and grilled by an array of formal and informal interest groups including labor representatives, parents, city political leaders, the teachers union, a business group focused on education, and various racial and ethnic coalitions and advocates. In the end all four applicants withdrew their candidacies. My hunch is that all four could see that the parts had pretty well eclipsed the whole, or even any notion of a larger whole. The candidates may have reached the conclusion that Gardner ventured when he said that "If leaders cannot find in their constituency any basis of shared values, principled leadership becomes nearly impossible."[3] I imagine that each of these four finalists concluded that there wasn't enough common ground on which to stand and from which to lead.

The problem of pluralism is felt most acutely by those at the pressure points of public leadership in our society: university presidents, school board superintendents, leaders of religious denominations, school principals, mayors, heads of not-for-profit groups, and others in similar leadership positions. It is no accident that the tenure for all such positions has grown remarkably brief. Among university presidents and school superintendents three years is a long time these days.

As the process for hiring our new school superintendent moved toward breakdown, the mayor and president of the city council intervened, urging that the process should be slowed down to allow more time for "community input." I thought that it was not perhaps more community input that was needed—we had plenty of that. What was needed was more community *output*. That is, we needed the various competing constituencies and interest groups to demonstrate some capacity to see the whole beyond the parts, to identify common objectives and a shared vision. That did not happen. The four candidates left town, shaking the dust from their shoes. The school board went to its default option of appointing the acting superintendent to a year's term.

This sort of thing is happening in many communities and in all kinds of institutions. The war of the parts against the whole is raging everywhere, though it is seldom a declared war nor even a noticed one. It is exacerbated by the fact that anyone who has an opinion is pretty well assured of getting a hearing, and often they win more than a hearing, perhaps even a certain legitimacy if they simply stand up and say, "I speak for so-and-so (e.g., teachers or parents or neighborhood residents)." Who knows if they actually do speak for those folks? We acclaim them willy-nilly. Often a group can exert a good deal of influence if they can claim a grievance, that their constituents have been left out or are underrepresented in the decision-making process. It sometimes seems that the quickest route to the moral high ground today is to claim the status of a victim. The end result of all this is a public discourse that often has the feel of an overcrowded nursery school on a bad day. Is it any wonder that candidates for leadership positions, after getting a clear picture of such a cacophony, are likely to say "thanks, but no thanks"?

What is to be done? How are we to avoid this kind of social balkanization? How are we to attract and retain decent and competent people to leadership positions when leadership is rendered nearly impossible by the conflict of competing interests and when leaders end up functioning only as referees? How are we to avoid the politicization of universities and school districts, not to mention schools and congregations?

To be sure, there are no easy answers, and leadership is always tough and often thankless. While the rancor of pluralism has been heightened in our own culture, this is not a completely new problem or challenge. The ancient Greeks struggled with it as the problem of the parts and the whole. They claimed, or at least Aristotle did, that the whole is more than the sum of its parts. The whole has its own reality, which deserves our respect and acknowledgment.

I recall learning this lesson, or having it brought home to me, in an unexpected place. I was a volunteer chaplain on an oncology team in a cancer ward at a large hospital. The team, which met weekly, was made up of half a dozen different specialists: nutritionists, social workers, chaplains, oncologists, nurses, and other professionals. We would discuss a series of patients, pooling our wisdom and sharing the responsibilities for their future care. Every now and again, the psychiatric social worker on the team asked, "How are *we* doing? How are we doing *as a group?*" She would often then add a wonderful phrase, "*The group has a life too.*" The group has a life too. There is a whole beyond our parts. It was easy to lose sight of that amid the pressing needs of patients, and amongst our various specialties and subspecialties. But it was a great point for us to ponder. The group has a life too. There is a whole beyond our parts. How is the whole doing? What are we contributing to the whole, to the group? Are we enhancing or diminishing the whole? Are we contributing to the life and vitality of the group, or simply drawing from it?

The apostle Paul offered a similar point when he developed his favorite metaphor for the church, the Body of Christ. Writing to the church in ancient Corinth, a Greek congregation that was divided into competing and hostile factions, Paul said, "Now you are the body of Christ and individually members of it" (1 Cor. 12:27). "For just as the body is one and has many members, and all the members of the body, though many, are one body, so it is with Christ" (1 Cor. 12:12). Paul went on to conjure the ridiculous picture of the foot that claims to be the whole body, or the ear or the head that claims not to be part of the whole body. "If the whole body were hearing, where would the sense of smell be?" (1 Cor. 12:17). "If the foot would say, 'Because I am not a hand, I do not belong to the body,' that would not make it any less a part of the body" (1 Cor. 12:15). If for the Greeks it was the struggle between the parts and the whole, for the New Testament it was the problem of unity and diversity.

In the past, and still today in some settings, unity has been allowed to eclipse diversity. Unity has meant uniformity. Today our problem seems the opposite, that diversity is overwhelming unity, or as Gardner put it, the war of the parts against the whole. Like that psychiatric social worker in the oncology team, Paul reminded a fractious congregation that their diversity was absolutely essential and God-given—the body needs its parts. But so too was their unity—the parts need the body. It is not an either/or but a both/and.

Constituents in a school district, university, or congregation cannot be content only to represent a specific and limited perspective and viewpoint, but they must also transcend that viewpoint to see the larger whole. Or as Paul put it to the Corinthians, "What I mean is that each of you says, 'I belong to Paul,' or 'I belong to Apollos,' or 'I belong to Cephas,' or 'I belong to Christ.' Has Christ been divided?" (1 Cor. 1:12-13).

Paul spoke of this as "discerning the body" (1 Cor. 1:29). Further on in his letter to the Corinthians he chastised them for their manner of celebrating the Lord's Supper or Communion. Paul noted that some members ate their fill of the bread and wine, so there was nothing left for the late arrivals, often the poorer members of the congregation. Paul scolded all those who ate and drank their fill "without discerning the body," which did not mean that they failed to see in the symbols of bread and wine the actual body of Christ, but rather that they failed to see one another. They were so caught up in their own needs, interests, and hungers that they did not see the needs of the social body, of the entire community.

Paul understood that it is often the least powerful and the most vulnerable who pay the price for this closed perspective. The noisy ones will probably get their due, but what of those who lack power or voice? One solution is, of course, to get them to the table and add their voices to the cacophony. That may be important, but it doesn't always work. More importantly, it doesn't address the real problem, which is the need of all participants to envision a common interest and a common good, one that keeps the most vulnerable in mind.

It is a lesson that families teach, or at least should teach. As children become teenagers they naturally develop a sense of themselves apart from their parents and family, and this is to be celebrated. Parents ought to want their sons and daughters to develop a sense of self, to individuate, as psychologists say. If it doesn't happen you're likely to have your kids living with you into their middle age. But this impulse to individuate often needs to be balanced by a sense of the value of family. Our children need to understand that while they are precious individuals, they are also part of a family. Too often today we seem to have lost this balance. It can sometimes seem today that children do not so much belong to a family, but that the family exists to serve children's needs and interests. It must, however, go both ways: you are special and you are a part of a family.

There was a long stretch of time that I spent working with chronically homeless people. After hours of listening, I realized that what many were telling me was, "I am a special person. I am a very special, unique individual." Often they thought of themselves as artists. Sometimes they considered themselves possessed of special spiritual gifts or insight. "I see things other people don't see," and so on. I was prepared to grant and affirm their specialness. What I noted, however, as I endured these long monologues was a frequent incapacity among some to also realize, "And you, aha!, are special too." The traffic was all one way. Some had become interpersonal black holes, taking in all that others might give, but without offering a thing in return, even so much as simply acknowledging the other person's reality and otherness.

The challenge to groups, institutions, congregations, and communities in our pluralistic time is the challenge of diversity and unity, of affirming the parts and yet seeing the whole beyond the parts. It is the particular task of leaders to name and articulate this challenge, and so find a workable truce in the war of the parts against the whole.

# GRIEVANCE
# GLUTTONY

S OME GUYS GET gadgets or hardware for Christmas. Others unwrap software or computer games. This old Luddite still gets books, and is happy for it. Among the new books in my Christmas stocking this year were the latest from William Sloane Coffin, *Credo*, and Gregg Easterbrook's *The Progress Paradox: How Life Gets Better While People Feel Worse*.

On my first riffle through each book I noted a common theme, the corrosive effect of nursing grievances. Coffin, a great one for the aphoristic turn of phrase, claims, "Nothing separates us more from God and our fellow human beings than our grievances. If you want to avoid God," says the onetime Yale chaplain, "concentrate on money, status, and health, but most of all on your grievances."[4]

Easterbrook, an editor for the *New Republic* magazine, is trying to figure out how it can be that when so many objective measures of health, well-being, and prosperity are on the up and up in the United States and Europe, so many people seem to be on the down and down. He thinks part of the answer is that we have become grievance gluttons. We love our grievances.

According to Easterbrook, "Trends in the educational, legal, political, and media systems all urge contemporary men and women to view themselves as wronged by various forces real and imagined; to get angry and fight back; to fixate on any harms of which they may have been the target; to search out wrongs about which to become outraged."[5]

Are not there many wrongs about which we should be outraged? Corporate greed and cooking of the books, forty-five million Americans without health care coverage, gross inequities in taxation, and more. Of course, there are reasons for outrage. But outrage ought to be used sparingly. The great psychologist Erik Erikson reminded us, "Do not misuse one of the strongest forces in life—true indignation in the service of vital values—to justify your own small self."

There is a difference between indignation in the cause of social injustice and nursing one's own grievances. The former tends to be animated by a concern for others and their welfare, and for a common good. The latter tends to cloak limited and often quite selfish concerns in the rhetoric of justice, fairness, or equity. It is one thing to be indignant about the lack of health care for poor children, but quite another to be mad as hell that your own co-pay has been raised five bucks. Today many seem unable to make that distinction.

The antidotes and alternatives to grievance gluttony are well known, if not so well or so often practiced. They include gratitude, forgiveness, and forbearance. Why, the words themselves almost sound antiquated.

Gratitude does not mean taking a naïve view of life. Nor does gratitude necessarily mean that one is showered with gifts or good fortune. It is more a matter of focus. According to Robert Emmons of the University of California, one of a new breed of scholars engaged in gratitude and forgiveness studies, "If you only think about your disappointments and unsatisfied wants, you may be prone to unhappiness." Whereas, if "you're fully aware of your disappointments, but at the same time thankful for the good that has happened and for your chance to live, you may show higher indices of well-being."[6] One might wonder if we really need a university professor to tell us this, but careful there, you're shading into the territory of a grievance!

Forgiveness is also eliciting new interest among scholars and social scientists. It turns out that practicing forgiveness is good for you, and that you're likely to get better at it as you get older. Easterbrook reports that a study at the University of Wisconsin found that older people are more likely to forgive than the young. He goes on to suggest that "the ability to forgive is a form of wisdom, learned through the passage of life."[7] Hey ho, aging boomers, there's hope for us yet!

The truth is that most of world's great religions have long known and taught the value of gratitude, forgiveness, and forbearance, the last of which might be defined in contemporary argot as "cutting others some slack." Those who insist on perpetuating the culture of complaint or on becoming grievance gluttons might contemplate Frederick Buechner's pithy observations about anger:

> *Of the Seven Deadly Sins, anger is possibly the most fun. To lick your wounds, to smack your lips over grievances long past, to roll over your tongue the prospect of bitter confrontations still to come, to savor to the last toothsome morsel both the pain you are given and the pain you are giving back—in many ways it is a feast fit for a king. The chief drawback is that what you are wolfing down is yourself. The skeleton at the feast is you.*[8]

# JESUS AND DARWIN

I DO ENJOY READING other people's bumper stickers—my recent favorite was "In the Event of Rapture, May I Have Your Car?" But I have not been one to display bumper stickers on my own car.

Why not? A combination of things. Maybe I'm a little shy. Besides that, I like to flatter myself that my views are sufficiently subtle and sophisticated that they cannot be easily summarized or reduced to the limited space of your average bumper sticker.

But that's all changed now. Recently I got a couple of fish: a Jesus fish and a Darwin fish. Immediately, I slapped them on with all the enthusiasm of a new convert. My two fish swim together on the milky, blue sea exterior of my Volkswagen Bug.

When I hit the road, it wasn't long before someone pulled alongside at a red light and commented, "What's the deal? It's either Jesus or Darwin, God or Evolution. You can't have it both ways. Take a stand!"

"I have," I answered back, "and this where I stand, four-square against dumb dichotomies and false polarities. I hereby declare myself dead set against pernicious either/ors, and all for both/ands. Both the book of Genesis and *The Origin of Species*. Surely, I am not the only one who thinks it possible to trust and worship God, and learn from science!"

In her 1998 study of public discourse, *The Argument Culture*, linguist Deborah Tannen observed, "The argument culture urges us to approach the world—and the people in it—in an adversarial frame of mind. It rests on the assumption that opposition is the best way to get anything done: the best way to discuss an idea is to set up a debate; the best way to cover news is to find spokespeople who express the most extreme, polarized views and present them as 'both sides.'"[9]

In such a culture, truth, which almost always eludes polarized extremes, is generally missing in action. Tannen offers a further useful distinction: "Public discourse requires making an argument for a point of view, not having an argument—as in having a fight."[10] The great Jesuit scholar and theologian John Courtney Murray is reputed to have said that, "a good argument is a great achievement." By "good argument" he did not mean half-truths heaved back and forth like hand grenades until our opponent has been bombed into submission. He meant the capacity to make a reasoned, sensible, and coherent argument for a point of view, and listening when and as others attempted to do the same for their point of view. *That* is a great achievement, and those who are able to pull it off are as endangered a species as the spotted owl and the California condor!

Contrary to those who claim the name of Christ and invoke as their slogan "Black or white, no room for grey," the Christian faith and its Scriptures are a wonderful display of complexity. In the Old Testament, for example, God is a God of righteousness *and* mercy, of judgment *and* compassion. As any conscientious parent or human being who is awake to life knows, the trick is to hold together in tension mercy and judgment, forgiveness and expectations, and find a way to honor both halves.

In the New Testament, a similar tension exists between faith and works. Paul says that faith (read: trust) is everything. James argues that "faith by itself, if it has no works (read: deeds), is dead" (James 2:17). Who's right? The church in its wisdom included both James and Paul in the Scriptures and in so doing said both are right. It's not either faith or works, it's both faith *and* works. You figure it out!

My own favorite illustration of this dynamic in the Bible comes from the Gospel of Luke, where the physician turned disciple lays the Parable of the Good Samaritan cheek by jowl with the story of Jesus' visit to the home of Martha and Mary (see Luke 10:25-42). The punch line, so to speak, of the Parable of the Good Samaritan is "Go and do likewise" (v. 37). That's also what Jesus says to the lawyer who wants to know who is his neighbor. But if you read on to the very next story, when Jesus visits the home of Martha and Mary, the punch line is essentially "sit and listen." Martha is grumpy because Mary isn't helping her clean up, but Jesus says Mary has chosen the better part. In so many words he tells Martha to sit and listen. After reading both, you may want to ask, which is it, go and do, or sit and listen? Luke tells us it's both. Go figure.

Creation or evolution, religion or science are only some of the silly but persistent either/or dichotomies of our day. Pro-life or pro-choice is another, even more pernicious one. After all, it is possible to be pro-choice and pro-life. Another one is the economy versus the environment. The either/or dichotomies abound, and they make good copy for the 11:00 P.M. news, but they make for poor public policy and a dumbed-down, if highly adrenalized, society. So it is in the realm of more personal ethical matters, where freedom and responsibility are presented as polar opposites, not halves of a whole truth.

In the religious realm, simplicity tends to be of two types. There is the simplicity that lies on this, the near side, of complexity. Those who embrace this simplicity dislike, seem frightened of, complexity. They prefer certainty to truth. There is, however, another kind of simplicity, the kind that is found on far side of life's complexities. It is this second type of complexity that is at the heart of Jesus' message, "Love the Lord your God with all your heart, . . . and love your neighbor as yourself" (Luke 10:27, NIV). This second simplicity resists reduction to a slogan or a bumper sticker, but it fits well in the frame of a good life.

I am starting a movement. Get a couple of fish for your car. (There are Buddha and Jehovah fish too.) Slap them on and you're a charter member of the "Both/And Society," which is not, by the way, a secret society. It's time to go public with this one!

# CITIZENS OR
# TAXPAYERS?

ERHAPS I AM not the only one to notice how often
the word *taxpayer* seems to be popping up in contemporary usage? Where we might once have used
the word *citizens* or *residents*, increasingly the default option is
*taxpayer*. Such language drift is often so subtle and gradual that
we miss it until it's too late. But subtle as it may be, it is also
significant.

One who has noted the shift, and commented upon it, is
Daniel Kemmis, the former mayor of Missoula, Montana, and
author of *The Good City*. According to Kemmis, "People who
customarily refer to themselves as taxpayers are not remotely
related to democratic citizens."[11]

Not long ago I thought of Kemmis's prickly observation as
I drove along the California coast. Every few miles there was
one of those signs announcing who was picking up the litter
and generally tending that section of the highway. The first
sign indicated the Baha'i faith was on the job. The next that
the good folks at the Transcendental New Science Center were
keeping the roadway tidy. A third announced that the Church
of Sacred Human Potential was responsible for the upkeep of
this section, at which point I muttered to myself that surely this
is California. But it was the fourth sign that tipped me over the

edge. It said simply, "A Concerned Citizen." Is this, I wondered, what we have come to? The concerned citizen is on par with esoteric religious sects? It could be.

Mayor Kemmis might not be surprised. "Taxpayers," he continues, "bear a dual relationship to government, neither half of which has anything to do with democracy. Taxpayers pay tribute to the government, and they receive services from it. So does every subject of a totalitarian regime. What taxpayers do not do, and what people who call themselves taxpayers have long since stopped even imagining themselves doing, is governing."[12]

Though Kemmis sounds like a public official who has spent too much time in front of community meetings being attacked by self-righteous and self-described taxpayers, his point is well taken. *Taxpayer* represents a diminished view of citizenship. A taxpayer pays taxes in expectation of receiving goods and services. A taxpayer is less a participant in governance or in the polis than a consumer of government services. Citizens, on the other hand, owe a certain loyalty to a city, town, state, or nation. To be a citizen is to enjoy both rights and responsibilities, benefits and obligations. It is to participate rather than consume. The last twenty years have seen the so-called taxpayer revolts, kicked off with California's famous or infamous Proposition 13, which spread like wildfire across most of the states. Is this an overdue curbing of government growth and spending? Or is it a de-funding of the public sector in the interests of private gain and a strategy to stoke the great furnace of the American economy?

In truth the debate between taxpayer and citizen is not a new one in our nation. Recall that the battle cry of the American Revolution was "No taxation without representation." Moreover, the Boston Tea Party, an icon of the Revolution, was a taxpayer's revolt. The taxpayer consciousness and its challenge to the more fulsome notion of citizenship has been with us for a long time.

At the founding of the nation two different strands of philosophy of the public good were especially pronounced. One was Enlightenment philosopher John Locke's notion of the social contract. According to Locke, individuals have emerged out of a state of nature to enter into a freely chosen but quite limited social contract. The social contract, the community, is the creation of sovereign individuals. The primary purpose of the social contract, according to Locke, is to protect private property. Thus, Locke is described as the philosopher par excellence of the theory of possessive individualism. As opposed to the rigid stratifications of the medieval world, in which society was understood as ordered by divine mandate, Locke's social contract emphasized individual property rights. Nevertheless, the crucial aspect of Locke's philosophy, and arguably the one perspective that was most influential on our nation's founding, was his conviction that the individual precedes the community. It is not difficult to see the Lockean lineage of today's taxpayer revolts and consciousness.

But the Lockean strand was not the only philosophy taking hold in the founding era. The other was carried to the new world by the Pilgrims and Puritans, among others. It was the more Hebraic and biblical notion of covenant. Though the social *contract* and the social *covenant* are both eight-letter words and do not seem all that different, they are birds of a very different feather indeed. If the individual precedes the community, as Locke believed, it is pretty much just the opposite in the biblical notion of covenant. Here it is the community that precedes the individual and forms the character of the individual. Moreover, while the social contract of Locke was a very limited arrangement, the social covenant derived from Hebraic thought was in many ways unlimited. It was charged with a sense of obligation to God and to one's neighbor that can be clearly heard in the words of the first governor of the Massachusetts Bay Colony, John Winthrop.

Aboard the *Arabella* in 1630 Winthrop gave his famous sermon, "A Modell of Christian Charity":

> *Now the only way to avoid this shipwreck, and to provide for our posterity is to follow the Counsel of Micah [the biblical prophet Micah], to do justly, to love mercy, to walk humbly with our God, for this end, we must be knit together in this work as one man [sic], we must entertain each other in brotherly Affection, we must be willing to abridge ourselves of our superfluities, for the supply of others' necessities, we must uphold familiar Commerce together in all meekness, gentleness, patience and liberality, we must delight in each other, make others' Conditions our own, rejoice together, mourn together, labor and suffer together, always having before our eyes our Commission and Community in the work . . .*[13]

If it is possible to see the lineage of the taxpayer movement in John Locke, another more communitarian perspective is equally evident here. If John Winthrop says, "We're all in this together," John Locke answers, "No, we're not." Citizens or taxpayers? Community first or individual first?

This debate plays out, or can be played out, in several kinds of social environments, including the family. Does an individual belong to a family? Or does the family exist in service of the individual? Likewise, it can be debated in terms of religious congregations and community groups. Is a person a member of such a congregation or group, sharing in both benefits and obligations and remaining faithful to it in bad times as well as good? Or do people come to religious congregations to get their spiritual needs met and stay only so long as it is working for them? And then to return to the original question, are we taxpayers who exchange money for services or citizens who participate in governing?

One major change since the founding of our nation has been the expansion of the free market and of a market mentality into all aspects of life. This development has tipped the scales and imperiled the balance between these two traditions, encouraging us to accept our role as consumers in all things, including things that cannot properly be consumed but only participated in, things like democracy, family, and faith. The covenantal perspective of the biblical prophets and the Pilgrims and Puritans has been overwhelmed by Locke's angry children. Though our taxes have been reduced, our common life has been diminished. Of course the answer does not lie in simply raising taxes, but in a different understanding of our role and in our relationship to one another. I think Winthrop captures that marvelously in his memorable phrase, "We must be willing to abridge ourselves of our superfluities in order to provide for others necessities." But I think I hear an objection. Is that you Mr. Locke?

# PROPHETS: TRUE OR FALSE?

EVERY COUPLE OF years I've turned the tables on my congregation. Instead of delivering a prepared sermon, I tell them it's time to "Quiz the Preacher." On three-by-five note cards I ask church members to write down a question they want to hear me answer—or at least one they want me to *try* to answer. The cards are usually collected by the ushers and brought forward. Then I shuffle the deck and deal myself a hand.

Every time I've done "Quiz the Preacher," I've gotten questions that are variations on this theme: How can we know the genuine article? What's the difference between a true and a false prophet? How do we know God's will? How can we tell if it's God's voice we hear or the voice of our fantasies or our fears? How in the world do we sort out the true prophets and leaders from the fakes and the charlatans?

In common usage *prophecy* is a confusing word. Popularly it is applied to those who are in the business of predicting the future. In the biblical tradition prophecy means something different. It isn't so much about predicting the future as it is about having insight into the present. Such insight ordinarily yields foresight, but foresight is to prediction as a poem is to a horoscope. While the latter intends to give you clues about the day or year ahead and your weal or woe in that same stretch of time, the former gives you clues about who you are, what life is and what it isn't, and about the world we live in.

The first of the Bible's prophets, Moses, addressed himself to the topic of prophets, which can be considered a type of leader or one of the attributes of a leader. First off, Moses warned the ancient Hebrews to give a wide berth to a whole category of future analysts and predictors. He reeled off a gaudy list of titles: diviners, soothsayers, augurs, sorcerers, charmers, mediums, and necromancers. Regardless of the specific title the job description is the same: predict the future, control the unknown, and manipulate divine or spiritual powers for security and gain. One summer evening at a street fair in Seattle, I decided on a lark to plunk down $10 to have my fortune told. If I had paid a lot more, I might have taken the whole thing much more seriously, which would have been a bad sign. Of course, many do pay more—a lot more. It was unnerving to learn that one of our former first ladies, Nancy Reagan, regularly consulted a San Francisco psychic before giving her blessing to the president's schedule!

It would be misleading, however, to lay all our skepticism at the door of card-carrying psychics and 1-800 soothsayers, even though that does seem to be a growth industry these days. Some soothsayers have more respectable titles, like market analyst and risk advisor. I was once changing my clothes in the locker room of a downtown athletic club when the television that hung on the wall mentioned the name Alan Greenspan, then chairman of the Federal Reserve. An elderly broker on the bench next to me perked to attention, saying, "Did Alan speak?" It sounded for all the world as if he had asked, "Is there a word from the Lord?" While the poor or the desperate knock on the door of Madame Chanya to have their palms read, many others are tuning in to *Wall Street Week* or studying the utterances of Chairman Greenspan as if they were analyzing arcane texts to predict the market and the future.

What is false prophecy? That which attempts to gain control over the future through the manipulation of divine or spiritual powers with the goal of ensuring and enhancing one's welfare and security, which generally comes at the expense of our neighbor's welfare and security. Most often, this sort of thing is shrouded in an aura of secrecy, special knowledge, or some other variety of insider trading.

What of the genuine article, the true prophet, the speaker of a message of truth and a trustworthy leader? Who are they and where do they come from? What do they do and say? And to what end?

When speaking of the true prophet, Moses told the Hebrews to keep their eyes open for someone like him. And who would that be? Would a true prophet have a square jaw, steely eyes, and broad shoulders? Charlton Heston in biblical getup? Arnold Schwarzenegger in armor? Not necessarily. A look at the story of Moses' call from God, as well as that of other of the biblical prophets, shows us one consistent trait: all were reluctant prophets. None wanted the job. None felt they were up to it or that they had what it took. Moses tried to beg off by saying that he was a lousy public speaker, afflicted with a chronic stutter. Jeremiah said he was way too young and that no one would take him seriously. Isaiah, when caught up in the presence of God, blurted out that he was a sinful man. It was the way they all began, by trying not to.

Not long ago a man came to see me who said that for some time he had felt something like a godly pull, a sense of God calling him in a particular way. But he found himself reluctant, hesitant, resisting, and responding with, "But God, this isn't a good time." He asked me, "If it were a genuine thing, wouldn't I embrace it readily, eagerly, and not be so reluctant?" "Au contraire, my friend," I said. "Every one of the Bible's prophets has a list of excuses a mile long. I regret to inform you that reluctance, far from being a disqualifier, is quite possibly the opposite. The ones I worry about, to tell you the truth, are those who aren't reluctant, who have no self-doubt and no hesitations." Or to put it another way, prophets and leaders who are in it for themselves, for fame or for glory, are not to be trusted.

If someone wants to be a priest or prophet, a teacher or therapist, a leader or a professor, to fill an empty place in themselves, watch out. Of course, we are all creatures full of mixed motives, and I, for one, probably became a minister because of some empty place in my soul. I became a better minister when I realized that no one else could fill that empty place but God, and that only I, with God's help, could do that. Reluctance is good, not bad.

A second thing Moses said about the genuine article is that God raises up his prophets from "among you," meaning from among the people and community. They are people who come from somewhere and who have a known address. In our society, we are big on the myth of the Lone Ranger, the masked stranger, the outsider who rides into Dodge, dispenses justice, and disappears into the sunset. And we tend to think of prophets as lonely figures, "voices crying in the wilderness." It is true that this kind of leadership and truth telling can be and usually is a lonely business. But that doesn't mean that genuine prophets or true leaders are people who burst on the scene from nowhere. On the contrary, they are people who have been nurtured in community, who have a tradition, a people, and a story. The Bible's prophets do not appear *ex nihilo* or come cloaked in the exotic and attended by special effects. They are hidden in plain sight, their disguise is their ordinariness. A prophet like Moses, Gandhi, Martin Luther King Jr., Dorothy Day, or Lech Walesa emerges from among the people, from the community. He or she is someone who knows what it is like to walk in your shoes because they are his or her shoes too. But isn't it true that a prophet is without honor in his own country? Indeed, it is. It is often a lonely business, but the point is he or she has a country!

But why the loneliness of prophets and, more generally, of leaders? That hints at another, a third quality, of the real deal, which is, they challenge their own. True prophets do not specialize in external enemies, in demonizing some "other." They tend, rather, to operate with Pogo's maxim in mind: "We have met the enemy and it is us." Or to quote from a somewhat more august authority, the leader of the Protestant Reformation, John Calvin: "Judgment begins with the house and people of God." The real prophets and genuine leaders tend to focus their challenges close to home, in fact, right among their own people, nation, church, or community. They don't name the sins and failures of the people on the other side of the world or across town or somewhere distant. They cause us to look at ourselves honestly. This is why we tend to honor prophets, if we ever do, after they are no longer with us. To be sure, prophets name evil, whether it is *segregation, oppression,* or *apartheid.* And they name evildoers. But just as often they challenge those on the short end of the stick to take hold of life and responsibility and not wait for someone else to deliver them.

A fourth indicator of reliable prophets is that they are less into predicting the future than they are into remembering the past, and specifically the tradition, story, and ideals of a people, a community, or a nation. The true prophet calls people to remember their deepest story and abiding values, and to be transformed by their power. Or to put it a somewhat different way, part of the reason true prophets tend to get into trouble is that they point out the gaps, the gaps between who we say we are and who we really are.

From the point of view of true prophets our biggest problem is not our inability to predict the future. It is our tendency to forget the past, to forget our story and who we are. Our problem is not that we lack the timetable for things to come. Our problem is amnesia. Prophets are radicals because they go back to the roots, which is the precise meaning of the word *radical*. They do what Martin Luther King Jr. did when he asked America if we meant what we said in our Declaration of Independence that "All men are created equal and endowed by their Creator with certain inalienable rights." The good ones, prophets that is, make the past present in order to create a genuine future.

The final characteristic of the true prophet that we ought to look for, of a leader who is authentic, is that they ask something of us, perhaps a great deal even. They don't let us off the hook, promising quick fixes or easy answers through the miracle of some technology. Nor do they offer the end to all our problems if we just get rid of some malefactor, whether it is Hutus, or Jews, or people who are gay or lesbian. They ask us to change, to grow, to give, to serve, to sacrifice, and to learn. Because of this, it's not easy having prophets around. They disturb us. But what they disturb us for and what they call us to is life. "The glory of God," wrote the early Christian teacher Irenaeus, "is a human being fully alive." True prophets are in the business of life, and of waking the dead.

# RACE AND REPENTANCE

A BILLBOARD ON JACKSON Street here in Seattle carries a public service advertisement for the upcoming Martin Luther King Jr. holiday. It shows four children and the caption reads, "Do you see an African American, a Caucasian, an Asian American, and a Hispanic? Or do you see four children? Think about it. January 19, Martin Luther King Jr. Day." But what is the right answer? Are those who drive by supposed to celebrate ethnicity, or are they to forget about it? Are we to be aware of our racial and ethnic diversity, or are we to be a color-blind society focused, as King said, not on the color of people's skin but on the content of their character?

Five decades after Brown vs. Board of Education, four decades after the Civil Rights Act of 1964, and nearly four decades since the assassination of King, it sometimes seems that race is more difficult to talk about and make sense of than ever before in America. Isn't it odd that despite all our good intentions, American society is in some respects more segregated than it was in the 1960s? Isn't it strange that we can-do Americans have been unable to fix or solve the race problem and that it continues to haunt us? "Why can't we," in the plaintive words of Rodney King, "all just get along?"

If television and the movies are to be believed, we not only all can get along, but we do. Several years ago I sat down with my daughter to watch a show that she was excited about. It was a sitcom about adolescents. What struck me most was the portrayal of race. In this show, there were young blacks and whites together. There were African American young men and women being as silly and contrived as their white adolescent counterparts. And all were the best of friends. The message seemed to be "Look, we all really do get along. They're just like us!"

Television has joined Hollywood in assuring us that this is the case. From the *Lethal Weapon* series of films starring Mel Gibson and Danny Glover, to *The Shawshank Redemption* starring Tim Robbins and Morgan Freeman, *White Men Can't Jump* starring Woody Harrelson and Wesley Snipes, to *The Little Princess* and a steady stream of others, Hollywood has offered us blacks and whites on screen who are best of friends. It is an appealing image.

In his recent book on the subject, *The Trouble with Friendship: Why Americans Can't Think Straight About Race*, Benjamin DeMott notes that America's problems with race appear to be solved, at least in the movies, one-to-one. Friendships in black and white, ebony and ivory, dominate the movies and tell us, like the television comedy I watched with my daughter, that we not only can, but do all get along. Hollywood seems to be telling us that it's the personal, not the political, that will save us.

But DeMott argues that such appealing screen and television images mask harsh realities. "Black infants die in America at twice the rate of white infants. One out of every two black children lives below the poverty line (as compared with one of every seven white children)." DeMott's sad statistical tale goes on: "Nearly four times as many black families exist below the poverty line as white families. Among youths under age twenty, death by murder occurs nearly ten times as often as among whites."[14] The number of black men who are or have been in jail is staggering, with the result that there are often five to ten times as many blacks as whites in prison, despite being a much smaller percentage of the overall population. The net worth of the typical white household is ten times that of the typical black household.

The fixation on the personal, on friendship, on the one-to-one promoted by Hollywood, is a comforting fiction. It miniaturizes and personalizes the more complex issues of social structures, public policy, and systems that we would rather not deal with. We prefer to examine our feelings, not our social policies. We tell ourselves, with a certain touching combination of pride and innocence, "I am not prejudiced," but we prefer not to look at social systems, institutions, and structures where racism endures and is perpetuated. It is another instance of the triumph of the sentimental. But what if racism is less about personal feelings than about social structures and history?

Not only do we prefer the personal to the political, or at least cinematic versions of the personal to the political, we generally seem disinclined to connect the dots between race and the steady dwindling of funding for the public sector that gathered momentum in the closing decades of the twentieth century. Is there a direct and demonstrable link between the waning of segregation and the de-funding of public education? Sometimes there is and sometimes there isn't. Is there a link to shifts in U.S. immigration patterns, following the major change in immigration law in the mid-1960s, shifts that have resulted in many more non-European immigrants and the so-called taxpayer revolts that began in the 1970s?

This revolt began in California, which recently became the first state in the nation, outside of Hawaii, to have a majority population of persons of color. It does not seem to me merely happenstance or coincidence that as the United States became a much more racially and ethnically pluralistic and diverse nation since about 1970, the many-faceted movement to reduce funds for public institutions and life has gathered force alongside a parallel drift toward privatization. One need not posit a simple cause-and-effect relationship to see a connection between growing racial diversity as well as the end of segregation and the pattern of diminishing funds for the public sector.

But the problem with Hollywood's emphasis on the personal and the one-to-one, an emphasis welcomed and echoed by not a few politicians, is that we don't really see much at all these days. We see what we want to see, that we are nice and well-meaning and that "they are just like us." As DeMott says, it is a comforting fiction. It is also what happens when we have no way to tell the truth about ourselves and our past. "Having no larger story that enables us truthfully to tell our story, we attempt amnesia,"[15] observes preacher Will Willimon, who is white and a southerner, as well as a Christian. In the Christian story of sin, violence, and redemption, Will found the resources he needed to face his own past as a white southerner whose family had owned slaves. He found there a story that names sin and evil accurately as well as a story that includes forgiveness and repentance. Apart from such a story, Willimon suggests, it is nearly impossible to be honest. We will accept Hollywood's comforting fictions about our present, and perpetuate our amnesia about our past.

It is a past that includes 250 years of slavery and 100 years of legally sanctioned segregation. The historian John Hope Franklin describes our history as "Filled with some of the ugliest possible examples of racial brutality and degradation in human history."[16] Of course, Americans have never been big on history. Henry Ford pretty well summed up the majority view when he declared that "history is bunk." But in this case, it may not be that the difficulty lies so much in perceiving the utility of history, as in coming to grips with a story of pain, brutality, and injustice that happens to be *our* story. How can we tell that story honestly? How can we all live together despite our past?

One of the things that my own conversion to the Christian faith has taught me is that apart from a larger story of forgiveness and repentance, a story of grace, all of us can become caught up in anxious and endless attempts at self-justification. We tell ourselves, "Well, I never owned any slaves," or "We're not like those other people, the prejudiced ones." Or we contend that we "have worked for everything we have," in order to deflect any suggestion that there are privileged groups and classes or privileged races. Apart from grace, honesty is nearly impossible. The apostle Paul never tires of reminding the early Christians that it's grace not self-justification that permits a new community to be established among strangers and enemies. Noting the well-known mantra of transactional analysis, "I'm OK, you're OK," someone quipped that the Christian equivalent might be "I'm not OK, you're not OK, but that's OK."

At present we seem determined to moralize and miniaturize the issues of race, to turn from the political and the historical to the personal and the sentimental. We lack a story and moral framework either large enough or deep enough to comprehend the complex reality of race in America and to guide us in facing both our past and our present. If it's not a problem that we can fix in a year or two with some new program, well then, forget it. Thus, we end up presenting ourselves to the world, not to mention to ourselves, not as people who have sinned and been forgiven, nor as a nation that has learned from its past, but as a people who are different from and better than others, which is, of course, neither true nor particularly endearing.

# IN A TIME OF WAR

O
N SUNDAY, SEPTEMBER 16, 2001, churches across the country were packed. The horror of 9/11 drove people to their knees and into the pews as no other moment in recent history. Americans experienced what theologian Paul Tillich called "the shaking of the foundation."[17] How have the churches responded to the crisis of 9/11 and to the subsequent war on terror? How have the churches in this country done in guiding their members and the nation?

Two new books have taken up these questions and come to quite different conclusions. Diana Butler Bass of Virginia Theological Seminary, and a former columnist for the *New York Times*, argues in her book *Broken We Kneel: Reflections on Faith and Citizenship* that what the churches have offered is more akin to "chapel" than "church."

"Waving flags and singing patriotic songs, many churches (after September 11) functioned as national chapels."[18] What the people who flooded into the pews on September 16 and subsequent weeks encountered was not so much, in Bass's view, the trans-national, trans-ethnic church and Gospel of Jesus Christ as it was a blend of the twenty-third Psalm and the National Anthem. Perhaps we ought not be surprised. For much of its history in this country, the Christian church, particularly the mainline Protestant churches, have been the custodian of an unofficial national religion. As the de facto established church, such congregations have long served to perform the functions of a chapel—to be there in crisis, to provide for people's religious needs, and to bless the nation's ideals and story.

However, there is a problem with chapel religion. Almost by definition chapel religion means you go (to church) when you need it, when you want a blessing or prayer for what you're up to, or when you wish to be married or have Mother buried. You go when you want to feel that God is *on* your side or at least *at* your side. Many call this church lite.

The word *chapel*, according to Bass, can be traced to France and the military. French kings housed the cape of their patron saint in a small temporary structure called a chapel. This chapel, with its relic inside, was carried into battle to ensure victory. Those who had responsibility for this chapel were called chaplains. Moreover, the *Oxford English Dictionary*'s definition of chapel is telling: it's defined as "any of a variety of buildings which in various ways is less than a church."

Bass argues that *church* is different than *chapel*. If *chapel* is a place or building where you expect to find a chaplain who will respond to your spiritual or religious needs, *church* is neither a building nor a social club. Church is something you are. "Church," writes Bass, "is a relational community reflecting God's Kingdom, established by Jesus Christ, birthed in the waters of baptism, fed with the bread and wine of Eucharist, and nurtured by practices of faith."[19]

In the wake of 9/11 Bass believes that American national needs and values eclipsed specifically Christian ones like peacemaking, reconciliation, and suffering evil rather than inflicting it. Bass's judgment is that chapel religion will not prove up to the challenges posed by the war on terror or radical Islam.

In many congregations across the country, the symbolic focal points of this debate have been two: church music and the American flag. Pastors and congregations have struggled over whether or not to sing songs like "God Bless America," which is really a Broadway show tune and not a hymn, or more hymnic offerings like "O Beautiful for Spacious Skies" and "My Country, 'Tis of Thee." The flag too has been a source of consternation. During the era of American Christendom it had become standard practice in many churches for the altar to be flanked by the Stars and Stripes on one side, and on the other side by a Christian flag, which is an historically recent creation. Such was the world in which I grew up, a world in which church and nation, God and country were woven together in one sacred fabric. The cross and the American flag together represented all that we held dear. For those who were formed by the era of American Christendom, which lasted until the mid- to late 1960s, to not display the flag in the church sanctuary is deeply troubling. But for Bass and others, this weaving together of cross and flag represents a failure to recognize a tension, a tension that Augustine long ago named as the tension between the City of Man and the City of God. Living during the decline of the Roman Empire, Augustine argued that while Christians have a responsibility to this earthly city, their ultimate loyalty is to the heavenly city. For at least some Christians today, America is viewed as a new Rome, an empire, and the church has proven better at being a chapel of the earthly empire than the outpost of the heavenly one.

"After 9/11, when many churches defaulted back to being state chapels," writes Bass, "did they miss the opportunity of a generation, the opportunity, that is, to be the church?"[20]

Jean Bethke Elshtain, a political philosopher at the University of Chicago, would probably agree with Bass's implied answer that the church missed a tremendous opportunity. But Elshtain believes the churches missed the opportunity in quite a different way and manner than that suggested by Bass. The title of Elshtain's book, *Just War Against Terror*, summarizes her argument that if ever the Christian doctrine of just war was applicable, it is certainly the case with America's war on terror. Moreover, she faults the churches and their leaders for their failure to call evil by its proper name in the wake of 9/11.

Elshtain, who is a Christian, recounts her own disappointment with the church on the Sunday of September 16. She found the message from the pulpit to be trivial and anemic. "All of us were in a state of shock," she writes. "We were looking for words of forthright encounter with what had happened and for guidance. But instead, we were told that 'It has been a terrible week. But that is no reason to lose your personal dreams. We need to hold onto our dreams!' Thousands dead in lower Manhattan and at the Pentagon and this was the best the minister could muster?"[21]

Elshtain's critique of the pulpit and the churches goes well beyond the particular sermon she happened to hear that day. Rather than naming evil for what it is, too many religious leaders after 9/11 rushed to rationalize the acts of terrorists as an understandable, if regrettable, response to poverty and injustice. While Bass thinks she witnessed the churches assume the position of national shrines and chapels, Elshtain believes a pseudo- or crypto-pacifism now dominates the pulpits of the mainline churches. Marks of this crypto-pacifism include the condemnation of all violence without any effort to make distinctions between intentional slaughter and ethical self-defense. To fail to make such distinctions, Elshtain argues, is equivalent to saying that a motorist who unintentionally kills a pedestrian is as culpable as a motorist who knowingly and deliberately runs

down a pedestrian. On 9/11, when innocents were intention-
ally killed, Elshtain believes that too many clergy and Christians failed to make this important distinction. Instead, church
leaders simply pontificated against violence of any kind.

Elshtain draws upon the legacy of Reinhold Niebuhr, one
of America's greatest theologians, to make her case. As the Nazis
rose to power in Germany in the 1930s, Niebuhr castigated
the pacifism and noninterventionism of many church leaders as
naïve and dangerous. There is a time when the use of force is
moral. From this perspective the question to be debated is *how*
to respond with restraint, not *whether* to respond at all. Just as
Niebuhr found in an earlier era, Elshtain finds in the church
today more interest in preserving its perceived purity than in
confronting evil. Like Niebuhr, Elshtain recognizes that in the
effort to confront and contain evil we might encounter guilt,
but this is no excuse for inaction.

Elshtain joins a reinvigorated debate on the doctrine of just
war, which has informed the church's thinking since Augustine. Like Darrell Cole in his recent book *When God Says War
Is Right: The Christian's Perspective on When and How to Fight*,
Elshtain argues that recent reformulations by the church of the
just-war tradition have set the bar so high for the ethical use of
force as to render the tradition useless.

Is there any common ground between Diana Butler
Bass and Jean Bethke Elshtain? Is there any common ground
between anti- and pro-war believers? It would seem hard to
find. And yet, both are arguing that the church needs to do a
better job of doing its homework, of speaking in its own native,
theological, and biblical tongue, and of knowing its own traditions and *raison d'etre*. For Bass the churches' voice has been
overlaid and nearly drowned out by nationalism. For Elshtain,

it has been garbled by a reflexive anti-Americanism. At least this much is true, in the wake of 9/11 and amid the war on terror, a renewed and important debate is underway about the role of the churches in America, and that is for the good.

# THE GAY DIVIDE

C AN WE TALK? Can we talk about homosexuality and the Christian faith? Not readily, it seems, not easily. Oh sure, we can talk with those who share our viewpoint, even our outrage, but as for talking with people whose views are different than our own and which challenge our own, why bother?

This summer we had a delightful young woman, a Whitman College student, living with us. She and her family are members of a congregation in Honolulu where I was once the pastor. One day I found her shaking her head in uncharacteristic frustration, even anger, as she read the newspaper. She was reading the letters to the editor in the wake of a recent King County court decision on gay marriage. "How can these people call themselves Christians? Why would I want to call myself a Christian," she asked, "when people who call themselves Christians say things like this?" She referred me to the letters expressing outrage at the judge's decision in support of marriage for persons who are gay or lesbian. "I just don't understand," she said, "how people can think that way!"

I have been the recipient of similar expressions of incomprehension and outrage, coming from the other side, the conservative side, when I have expressed an accepting view on homosexuality. "How can you call yourself a Christian?"

wrote shocked and offended fellow believers. "It is ministers like you who are responsible for the downfall of the church and of this country!"

Can we talk? We Christians stand at a distance and shout, but we do not talk. There are other questions as well, questions that must perplex people outside this faith and religion, as well as those inside it. Namely, how can people who profess the same faith come to such different conclusions about homosexuality? Moreover, what is the basis for their very different views?

As for the first question, how can people of the same faith hold such divergent views? That probably shouldn't be so surprising. All the great religions are complex, not simple. They are multilayered affairs with long histories and with different expressions and traditions. They do not speak in a single voice. While this may be frustrating, the complexity is more likely a strength than a weakness. Simplistic answers too often come from ideological movements, in which members speak with a single voice.

Yet how do people of the same faith, Christians in this instance, come to such different conclusions? Those who oppose the inclusion of persons who are gay and lesbian in church and society, and who are disturbed by gay marriage, point to five passages of the Bible where same-gender sexual behavior is condemned: two passages in the book of Leviticus, three in the letters of Paul. Given these texts and the long history of the opposition by the church to homosexual behavior, opponents argue that the burden of proof that homosexuality is not a sin lies on those who now advocate change.

On the other side of the issue are those who support the inclusion of persons who are gay or lesbian in church and society, following the example of the inclusive ministry of Jesus.

They note that Jesus frequently kept company with those of his own time who were considered unclean or beyond redemption by the good, religious people. Jesus went to the lepers, the prostitutes, and the tax collectors (who collaborated with Rome), and included them in his company. He spoke of the hated Samaritans as good. In what is perhaps his best-known parable, of the Good Samaritan, he depicts those of his own faith as falling short, while a despised Samaritan exemplified faith's compassion. Given the inclusive ministry of Jesus, along with the fact that Jesus himself said nothing specifically about homosexuality, supporters of tolerance argue that those who would exclude gay and lesbian persons from the church need to reconsider their justifications.

Liberals on this issue say that the Scriptures cited by the opposition are relatively few and hardly central to the core of the faith. Conservatives accuse liberals of cherry-picking the Scriptures and discarding what they don't like. Liberals say that the Bible, a book written in a different time and place, knows nothing of what today is called sexual orientation, that is, that some percentage of people in every culture and population are sexually oriented to those of their own gender. They point to recent studies indicating that there is a genetic component to sexual orientation.

Conservatives reply that what they refer to as the homosexualist movement is an effort to redefine nature and its limits. They contend that sexuality is more a matter of nurture than nature, and that the more society accepts and legitimizes homosexuality, the more homosexuality there will be. Back and forth go the arguments and charges, drawn from Scripture, from tradition, and from psychosocial studies. Is there hope for finding any common ground? Or must we simply agree to disagree and live, as with so many other issues, in our polarized camps?

I remember Gertrude, an older woman in the first church I served as pastor. Back then, nearly thirty years ago, the issue of homosexuality was already creating controversy, though in a slightly different way. Then the question was whether the church would support civil rights and legal protections for gays and lesbians. Gertrude wasn't so sure that supporting equal protection for gays in housing and jobs was a good idea. "I've read about these homosexuals," I recall her saying, "the kind of lives they lead. It's not good." In response I asked her if she knew Joel, another member of the congregation. "Oh yes, Joel, what a nice boy," she answered. "Well, Joel," I said (with his permission), "is a gay man, a homosexual." "Really," said Gertrude, obviously surprised, even shocked. In some confusion she continued, "But Joel is such a good member of the church. We've known his family a long time. They are good people." A month or so later Gertrude said to me, "I've decided that if Joel is a homosexual, then it's OK." "What's OK?" I asked. "Well, being gay," said Gertrude.

Such a story may be thought sentimental, but in my experience as a pastor it is the way that people come to a different conclusion. Not by debating the issue as social policy or even on the basis of Scripture, but because they know someone who is gay or lesbian and it is evident to them that this person is a wonderful human being and a good Christian. As someone said to me just the other day, "I grew up as a quite conservative Christian, but in graduate school two of my teachers were gay men. They were both extraordinary human beings and wonderful Christians. I just couldn't see how God could hate them or their lives. In fact, watching one care for his partner, who was dying of AIDS at the time, I witnessed extraordinary, Christ-like devotion and sacrifice."

Not only does such personal experience seem persuasive to many, but there is evidence of something very much like this in the Bible itself. Often overlooked in the debate about homosexuality is the controversy in the early church and in much of the New Testament of the inclusion of non-Jews, the Gentiles. Like Jesus himself, the early followers of Jesus were Jews. As these early followers fanned out into the world beyond Israel, the church faced a challenge. Could non-Jews, Gentiles, be admitted into the emerging church? Could you be a Christian without the mark of the covenant, namely, circumcision?

Scripture argued clearly and decisively, beginning in Genesis, on the importance of keeping the rites and rituals of Judaism, including circumcision. Yet in the New Testament, particularly in the Acts of the Apostles, the story of spiritual experience supersedes the Bible, *in the Bible itself.* At the famed Jerusalem Council of the early church, Paul and others report that "the gift of the Holy Spirit had been poured out even on the Gentiles" (Acts 10:45). God, proclaims an astonished Peter, is doing a new thing. Perhaps this is an analogy that Christians need to consider in the contemporary debate on homosexuality. It shows the early church "doing a Gertrude," so to speak.

Even if this analogy is not convincing, and I know it won't be for many, there may be one further point to be directed to all of us in the currently polarized debate. I have a friend who organizes his paperwork on all types of matters and questions that require a decision into three piles. There is the pile for *Accept,* and the pile for *Reject*—no surprise there. But he also has a third possible category that he calls *Awaiting Further Light.* It seems to me that people of faith, who by definition know that God is God and they are not God, and that they therefore lack the full, complete, and absolute Truth, have good reason to file some issues under category *Awaiting Further Light.* This approach to the contemporary debates on homosexuality, as well as other issues, might encourage our capacity to listen, to listen to views not our own. If there is one quality that should characterize faith and religious people in our day, my own vote is for a greater measure of humility.

# TECHNOLOGY AND
# HUMAN VALUES

OR MY FIRST teaching job I was the entire social science department of a vocational-technical community college in Hawaii. I was hired, just before the term began, to teach two sections of a class called "Technology and Human Values" to budding beauticians, plumbers, auto mechanics, and cooks. The class came with a textbook, actually a reader. It portrayed technology in the spirit of the times, the early seventies, as an impersonal demonic force. "Great," I thought to myself, "I'm supposed to tell kids who have been studying their respective technical fields for two years that technology is the Great Satan. No wonder the person who had this job before me disappeared!" But the questions implied in the course title were important. How has modern technology affected our culture? What are its blessings and its curses? Does it enhance or diminish human character? And why hasn't technology quite fulfilled its utopian promise?

In its myriad manifestations, technology is the handmaid and DNA of modernity and its great quest to get things under control. As I write these words the days are growing shorter and temperatures are drifting downward. In a week or two our furnace will kick in, signaling that fall is here and winter on its way. I will be glad, if I even think about it, that we have central heating. While I sometimes enjoy chopping wood and like to make a fire in the fireplace, I wouldn't like any of it if it were the principal means of heating our home. Chopping wood, not to mention finding it, and building fires would get old fast. So, thank goodness for the furnace. Thanks for the good, complicated tool called central heating.

But let us note, as the philosopher Albert Borgman does in his several books on technology, some changes that attend such modern miracles as central heating and of which we should be mindful. Borgman goes deeper on technology and values than the common and simpleminded depiction of it as either Savior or Satan. He points out that technology means "reducing the burden" of domestic chores, such as wood cutting, wood gathering, and fire building. But Borgman suggests that we ought not want to lessen the burden in *all* cases. At least sometimes, something of value may be lost when the burden is reduced or eliminated.

Let's consider a different example, say, music. If one wants music, it's really no harder than central heating. It may not kick on automatically, but of course it can if you choose to spend the money. At any rate, with radio and compact discs, not to mention audio systems and home entertainment centers, music is convenient, accessible, and obtained with relative ease. Flip a switch or push a button. Voila, music. Amazing, really.

Contrast this technological delivery of music with something different or a different way of producing music, such as learning to play the violin. Learning to play the violin is neither convenient, nor is it easy (especially if it's me who's learning). It is demanding and difficult. It requires persistence and practice, resolve, and hours of repetition. It is what Borgman calls a high-threshold activity. The threshold of learning to create music with a violin is incredibly higher than it is for turning on a CD. The higher threshold is made up of many things: finding and taking lessons from a teacher, practicing for many hours, learning a new language and vocabulary, participating in a discipline, and meeting the standards of the community of violinists and musicians. It becomes harder to sustain this kind of discipline and disciplined activity in the face of technology, which may be one reason why our technical proficiency seems to be increasing simultaneously with a general dumbing down of the culture.

The point is that sometimes we ought to want this higher threshold because it yields greater rewards in terms of relationships, character, personal development, and contribution to the community. Technology tends to lower such thresholds or to eliminate them altogether. Moreover, we become accustomed to technology's implicit values: convenience, ease, accessibility, and speed. We tend to think that's the way it is supposed to be in all areas of life. An exchange between characters in a recent movie captured it perfectly: the first character says, "What you want is immediate gratification!" and the second answers, "No, that's not soon enough."

In a society as technologically proficient as ours, we have become less tolerant of inconvenience, of activities that demand a great deal of us, and of those pursuits that require patience and resolve. These types of pursuits include marriage, raising children, developing proficiency in an art or profession, and all aspects of the political process. During a benefit for a homeless shelter held in the swank banquet room on the 107th floor of a skyscraper, I prayed, "It is odd, Lord, that we can manage to build a magnificent building like this and have such a splendid lunch here, and yet we seem unable to know how to solve the problems of homelessness on the streets so far below us."

Building such a building is a technical feat. Dealing with homelessness is a political problem.

As another example, let's consider voting. I like the motto "Voting is a Civic Sacrament." I enjoy going to the polling place at the nearby elementary school, visiting with the poll workers and seeing a neighbor or two, and punching my ballot. Voting does have a sacramental, or at least ritualistic, feel. In recent years we have seen attempts to universalize voting by mail, and I expect it won't be long before we're voting at computer screens or on our home computer. Such steps, I can imagine, will prove both helpful and appealing in many ways. But something shall be lost in the process of lowering the threshold to make voting more accessible, more convenient, in order to provide quicker election results. The human interaction, the sense of community, the ritual of it shall be sacrificed to greater ease, convenience, speed, and accessibility, as well as the claim of greater accuracy through machines. These are values that are beyond question, at least at present, in our culture. Borgman's reflections help us to get a handle on the ambiguity of technology and on its implicit values of ease, accessibility, convenience, and quickness. It is simply too easy to portray technology as either the key to better living or the thing that dehumanizes us all. But when we celebrate its blessings (remember the furnace) we must also come to grips with the consequences of technology and the infiltration into our culture of its implicit values: accessibility, ease, convenience, quickness, and instant gratification.

For reasons that remain a mystery to me, my wife has always been dead set against dishwashers. So we always wash dishes by hand in the kitchen sink. It turns out that there are some corollary benefits of this higher threshold activity. For example, doing the dishes is a great way to get your hands really clean if you've been working on a car. Moreover, as a more or less mindless thing it allows a certain form of contemplation. And, finally, if others are around and you can talk them into drying, the whole enterprise seems to be a great setting for conversation. Doing the dishes by hand carries a higher burden but also greater rewards. This may explain why more technology does not always lead to happier and fuller lives, despite the promise that it would.

And there's one more aspect to consider. Without much clear thinking, we often assume that most every challenge we face as human beings and societies is amenable to a technological solution. Actually, very few of the most important challenges we face today lend themselves to a technological solution. As an example, take health care. We tend to view health care as a technical matter. If we develop more and better medications, diagnostic tools, and surgical procedures, and so on, we think we shall solve our problems. But millions of Americans, forty-five million at last count, have *no health care coverage*. This is not a technical problem nor will it be solved by technical means. It is rather a community problem, a political and moral problem that can only be addressed by change in the hearts and minds of people. In my experience, that kind of work is slow, difficult, and costly. It is seldom convenient, quick, or readily accessible. And yet without a change of heart, all the most advanced medical tools and techniques in the world shall not save us.

Moreover, one might very well make the argument that technological innovations in the medical field are more the problem rather than the solution. As costly and increasingly sophisticated medical interventions become available the overall costs of basic medical care are driven higher, with the result that a minimum level of care is out of reach for many. Beyond that, so much of medical technology is devoted to end-of-life care and intervention, rather than preventive care and health, which usually requires little technology but does requires more discipline. In these ways technology amplifies, rather than reduces, inequity. The moral and political question then arises: Will broad accessibility and relative equity of care be our goal, or will health care look increasingly like flying? That is, you can fly first class, business class, or coach. Or you can simply stay on the ground.

Our technological proficiency is both a strength and a weakness. Accustomed to ease and immediacy, we grow lazy. Seduced into thinking all problems have a technical solution, we become intolerant of the slow, difficult, and costly work that builds human communities and addresses political problems. Our technological prowess can blind us to the beauties and rewards of simple acts like joining our fellow citizens at the polling place, practicing piano, and washing dishes at the kitchen sink.

# HOLY STORIES

ARE THE BIBLE'S stories true? At a certain age, children will ask of a story, "Is that a true story? Did it really happen?" We moderns tend to define *truth* and a *true story* based on whether it really happened, whether it is verifiable according to the canons of evidence and modern historical study. But to me that seems a limited and limiting understanding of truth. Many of the biblical stories are less concerned with the truth of fact than the truth of meaning. It is not that they are merely fanciful. All have roots in actual history, human culture, and experience, but it isn't a narrow truth based on *facts alone*. It is more.

The Native American teacher Black Elk was getting at the difference when he remarked of the stories of his people, "Whether it happened so or not, I do not know; but if you think about it you can see that it is true." Of course, history does make clear that some stories have been a blessing while others have been a curse. Some stories deceive and mislead (Adolf Hitler's *Mein Kampf* comes to mind), while others correct and deepen. What's the difference? What makes a story truthful?

For openers, truthful stories do not admit of only a single meaning, interpretation, or moral. They do not tell us what to think. They enable us to see, and to see more than we saw before. They have a spaciousness and depth, a capacity to yield different meanings and truths, as well as to provoke a deepened search for meaning and truth. The Bible's stories are evocative and not moralistic. To say that such stories cannot be reduced to a single and fixed meaning or interpretation does not mean they are infinitely malleable, or that they can mean whatever you want them to mean. No, they have a direction and shape, one that opens the world rather than closing it.

This came as a surprise to me when I began to study the biblical texts seriously. Somehow I had imagined that they were mostly moral example stories and accounts of morally exemplary figures. A sort of really big Book of Virtues. Imagine my surprise when I read the Abraham and Sarah stories for the first time, and found an Abraham quite willing to do what it took to save his own skin. He was a tower of strength at one moment, but in the very next ready to jeopardize his own wife, not to mention God's great project. Worried that Pharoah might kill him to take his wife, Abraham lied to Pharoah, telling him that Sarah was his sister. A chapter or two later it is Egypt's Pharoah who will lecture Abraham on ethics. The point, it seems, is that the unfolding story of the Bible is less about the perfections or imperfections of its human characters than about a strange and mysterious God who is determined to work with and through imperfect human beings.

This is a truthful story because it tells us the truth about ourselves, namely, we are a mixed bag. We are capable of great courage and great cowardice. We do wonderful things, and we do things that are selfish and terrible. And it tells another truth as well: Despite our own flaws and failures there is a gracious power, sometimes hidden and sometimes revealed, steadily at work for good and healing in the world. If we give it half a chance it will work through us. When we don't give it a chance, it keeps on anyway.

Then you come to Moses and learn that the great liberator and lawgiver began life as a great hothead and a murderer, and that the burning bush incident unfolded during Moses' self-imposed exile and flight from the law. It continues like this: Jeremiah protests that he is too young to be any sort of prophet; Esther must choose between the security of the palace of Israel's conqueror, where her Jewish identity is hidden, or fighting for her own people and risking their fate; Ruth, the foreigner from Moab who through a strange and racy tale becomes the grandmother of Israel's King David; and on down through the stories of Saul, the former Christian persecutor who became Paul, certainly the most influential figure in the New Testament after Jesus himself.

Paul would speak of himself as "the least of the apostles" and as "one untimely born" (1 Cor. 15:8-9). And it wasn't false modesty—it was an acute self-awareness. As Saul, he was a self-righteous and angry zealot, bound and determined to stamp out the little band that followed Jesus. Nevertheless, this very Saul is decked by the light on the Damascus Road. Just when readers are cheering and saying, "Yeah, God, bust his chops," God announces that Saul will be called Paul and is God's odd and surely unexpected choice to bring the faith and story of Jesus to the Gentile world. And the crowd gasps, saying, "No, God, anybody but him." We prefer our enemies skewered, not saved.

These were not, I realized, stories about good little boys and girls, but about real people, ragged and raw. Moreover, they were stories about God. Everywhere here an elusive yet intrusive and disruptive God was the main character. These were stories of people as mixed and mottled as I knew myself to be, who encountered a strange and persistent deity and were called to some great task in their time. All the stories had a moral meaning and dimension, but they did not reduce the complexity and mystery of life in ways that were moralistic. Thus, truthful stories show us the enormous costs, as well as the rewards, of virtue and courage. Truthful stories insist that there is moral meaning, that is, that our own choices and actions do matter, but they do not insist on simple moral equations or easy correlations of virtue and reward, sin and punishment. Life is not that simple.

True stories, which I believe the Biblical stories to be, are not reductive but evocative. They admit of more than one meaning or interpretation. Such stories have moral meaning but are not moralistic. True stories do not locate all that is false and evil in our enemies, whoever they may be. They reveal us to ourselves, showing us both our own evil as well as our capacity for goodness. They do not simplify life to an easy calculus of rewards and punishments. They respect life's complexity. Moreover, these stories hold in tension great overarching and often conflicting themes, such as purpose or providence on one hand, and human freedom on the other.

Beyond spaciousness, evocative capacity, and their resistance to moralizing, the stories of the Bible hold in unresolved tension certain great themes or convictions, such as design and free will, divine plan and human responsibility. In his wonderful book *The Art of Biblical Narrative*, Robert Altar argues that it is the distinctive genius of the biblical story to never resolve itself in favor of either pole in the design versus free will debate, but to hold the two in constant and unresolved tension. Thus in the great novella about Joseph, which concludes the book of Genesis, Joseph tells his brothers, "Even though you intended to do me harm, God intended it for good" (Gen. 50:20). That is a grand design, a plan, and a purpose unfolds in history and in the sordid struggles and deceptions in that one conflicted family. But their choices were, at one and the same time, their own. Joseph's brothers, though they were forgiven, are nevertheless responsible for casting him into a pit to die and then selling him into slavery. The Genesis story and the entire biblical narrative affirm a redemptive purpose at work in history, but it is one that respects human freedom. Such a tension cannot be easily held conceptually, but it can be sustained within the frame of the story. There are other truths held in tension besides divine plan and human freedom. There are faith and works, as well as judgment and mercy. For a society given to choosing and engaging in perpetual pitched battles over partial truths (pro-life versus pro-choice comes to mind), this could be instructive.

In the end what is most important is this: the stories of Scripture and all true stories have the capacity to change us, to make us different and better, and maybe even to make us new. When I was a child the civil rights movement was fueled by the great black preachers of the day and their telling and re-telling of the biblical stories in a way that changed lives and changed a nation. These stories compelled the unarmed and defenseless to march, sit down, and stand up in protest. These stories framed our own era in the grand story of the struggle for human freedom and dignity. The stories challenged us and they changed us.

It seems one of the great diminishments of modernity that we have become, for the most part, a people without a story. Oh, we have our personal and family stories, which are good but not enough. We supplement those with stories of different cultures and ethnic groups. All sorts of stories are being told in the various media and on television, but most of them are only camouflage for the story of consumer capitalism and its promises of a purchased peace and happiness. We need a larger story, and much of my life as a pastor has been dedicated to furnishing the imaginations of people in my congregations with such stories, the story of the Bible.

In the early pages of her novel *Ceremony*, the Native American author Leslie Marmon Silko writes, "I will tell you something about stories . . . They aren't just entertainment. Don't be fooled. They are all we have, you see, all we have to fight off illness and death. You don't have anything if you don't have the stories."[22] Do you have the stories?

# WHO ARE THOSE CHRISTIANS?

FOR SOME TODAY, all Christians are closed-minded religious bigots whose politics are somewhere to the right of the Attila the Hun. For others, Christians can be explained in terms of the two-party theory: there are liberal and progressive Christians on one side and conservative and evangelical Christians on the other. Both explanatory frameworks are inadequate to convey the diverse and complex reality of Christianity in America today. Like much else in postmodern America, the situation is wonderfully messy. It doesn't lend itself to neat explanations or to a simple duality of liberal and conservative. Postmodernity is transgressive, that is, given to crossing boundaries. So today you have progressive evangelicals, theological postliberals, the new orthodox, as well as ancient-modern Christians. Such stereotype shattering and boundary crossing strikes me as promising.

What follows is an attempt to make sense of it all with different categories and descriptions. Such categories are what the great sociologist Max Weber called "ideal types." In reality, things are often more complex and some readers will object that they don't fit in any category. And they will be right. Still, the following taxonomy of Christians in twenty-first-century America has value, if only to overcome even less accurate explanatory frameworks such as those above. Let's take a crack at surveying the landscape with five large categories: mainline, evangelical, fundamentalist, charismatic, and Catholic. We might add a sixth category, namely, the Orthodox in America. Orthodoxy is a small but growing presence in North America, one characterized by rich iconography and colorful liturgy. It is a visual culture that will, I predict, grow in twenty-first century North America.

Mainline Christians are the Protestant Christian denominations that came from Europe during the colonial period and were for centuries the dominant churches in the United States. The mainline Christians include long-established groups like American (Northern) Baptists, Congregationalists (now United Church of Christ), United Methodists, Presbyterians, and Episcopalians. Today most Lutherans probably fit in the mainline category, although for some years Lutherans were seen, like Catholics, as a church of immigrants.

One broad-brush way to differentiate the dominant Christian groups is to identify how they relate to modernity, or what some call "The Enlightenment Project," with its hallmark values of reason, progress, optimism, individualism, and tolerance. Mainline Christians have been open and receptive to modernity, working to accommodate Christianity and modernity. By contrast, fundamentalists circled the wagons against modernity, which they perceived as a threat. In between, evangelicals and Catholics took a more nuanced view, sometimes affirming but often rejecting the varied manifestations of modernity and its challenge to traditional culture and values.

The mainline Christian openness to modernity, even embrace of it, means that mainline Christians don't typically see a conflict between religion and science, faith and evolution. Moreover, mainliners view other religions as valid. They have welcomed historical and critical approaches to studying the Bible. Often, but not always, mainliners speak of Jesus as "a way, not the way." Because of their historic presence and predominance in the United States, mainliners have typically played important roles in American society, such as being the conscience of the community, the instrument of aid to the least fortunate, or as centers of community life. In recent decades mainline churches have lost market share, partly because they did not retain the allegiance of the huge baby-boomer generation that had been raised in mainline congregations in the 1950s and '60s. For that generation, personal choice and individual spiritual seeking proved more important than institutional or brand loyalty.

During the late nineteenth and early twentieth centuries, while mainliners were busy embracing modernity, science, and critical methods for studying the Bible, fundamentalists were alarmed and threatened by the very same things. The reliability and authority of the Bible, along with the authority of the family and traditional values, seemed under assault. Fundamentalism emerged, not as many imagine, long ago but in fairly recent history. Most would date it to the 1920s, when the modernist-fundamentalist conflict arose over newer methods of studying the Scriptures as well as Darwinian theory. In more recent years, fundamentalists have been galvanized by a series of social changes that they feared signaled the vanishing of traditional America: the outlawing of school prayer, legalization of abortion, the rapid rise and acceptability of divorce, and changes in traditional roles of men and women. In the face of these threats, as well as ones that were more theological in nature, fundamentalists delineated "the Fundamentals," which included the virgin birth, the divinity of Christ, and the literal and inerrant truth of the Bible.

It has long been the prevailing assumption among secular people and scholars that fundamentalism was on the wane and it was only a matter of time until it would shrivel up and die. On the contrary, fundamentalists in the United States (as elsewhere in the world, see Islamic fundamentalism) have been building institutions, schools, colleges, and agencies as rapidly as mainline Christians have been losing their own similar networks over the last fifty years. Moreover, fundamentalists have taken to modern communication technology like ducks to water, probably because theirs is primarily an oral, not a written, culture. It is mostly fundamentalists and their cousins, charismatics, who show up on cable television. For much of its life, fundamentalism has been in a fighting mood, quick to name and protect the boundaries. Of late, the line between fundamentalism and evangelicalism is a little harder to determine because fundamentalists, who have historically been about doctrine and dogma, are also about personal transformation. If you see the words *Bible Believing* or *Bible Church* in a church name, it's a good bet it will be fundamentalist. Many are independent, some are various forms of Baptist.

In between the more modernity-embracing mainliners, on one hand, and the modernity-averse fundamentalists, on the other, are the evangelicals. Unlike the fundamentalists, whose leading concern has been doctrine, evangelicals have been focused on transformation and changing lives. This has proven particularly fertile ground in the last forty-plus years, a time of rapid cultural change, as well as family disarray spurred on by divorce and widespread drug and alcohol abuse and addiction. Many lives have skidded off the rails, creating a climate receptive to radical redirection and personal change.

You won't find evangelicals going to the mat over a doctrine in quite the way of fundamentalists, but you will find them very concerned about a personal relationship with Jesus Christ that changes a person's life. While most evangelical Christians voted Republican in the last two elections, there are significant elements within evangelical Christianity that are oriented to what has been thought of as the causes of liberal and mainline Christians, for example, the plight of the poor, eradication of hunger, abolition of capital punishment, feminism, as well as environmental issues. Hence, you have "progressive evangelicals." Moreover, the sense of being under cultural attack, often acute among fundamentalists, is less true of evangelicals who are increasingly more at home in contemporary culture. You will find evangelicals in the historic mainline groups, like Presbyterians, as well as more characteristically evangelical groups like Free Methodists, Church of the Nazarene, and Southern Baptists. Many newer independent or "community churches" are also evangelical.

Most of the predominately African American churches, a vibrant part of the Christianity in the United States, are evangelical, meaning they emphasize transformation and a personal relationship with Jesus Christ. At the same time, many African American churches often find common cause with mainliners and progressive evangelicals on social and political concerns.

A large and growing subgroup of evangelical Christianity is charismatic Christians. Charismatics share an experience they describe as the gift of the Holy Spirit, often expressed by "speaking in tongues," or ecstatic speech, and emotionally charged or expressive worship. Like fundamentalism, charismatic Christianity in this country dates to the early part of the twentieth century and up until fairly recently was more at the social margins than in the mainstream. Of late, some charismatic denominations, like the Assembly of God as well as newcomers like the Vineyard Churches, have shown very dramatic growth and movement into the social mainstream. Like evangelicals, charismatics are conversion oriented. They go on to embrace the gifts of the Holy Spirit, not only in ecstatic speech but in prophecy and healing.

Historically, there has been tension, even ill will, between fundamentalist and charismatic Christianity. Partly, it arises from their competing for the same sociological share of the market, typically less affluent white Americans. Moreover, where fundamentalists like to keep worship pretty well tied down, charismatic Christians revel in worship that's open and loose.

And what of Roman Catholicism, the largest single church in the country? The short answer or description is that Catholicism includes all of the above categories, including more liberal elements that are in synch with Protestant mainliners, evangelical and charismatic churches, as well as traditionalist Catholics, who are Catholicism's version of fundamentalists. This latter group is generally dismayed at most of the changes brought about by the Second Vatican Council, which marked Catholicism's embrace of modernity. It has been a characteristic strength of Catholicism to hold under one very large tent a great variety of movements and experiences; however, other changes make this a constant challenge today. There a serious shortage of trained clergy, the recent sex abuse scandals involving priests have left the church reeling, and a huge shift in the ethnicity of Catholicism in the United States is underway. The Catholic Church in the United States was once predominately the church of the Irish, Italians, and Eastern Europeans, but today the face of Catholicism is changing dramatically with the huge immigration influx of Hispanics and Asians.

Where does this leave us? Clearly, not all Christians are conservatives or right-wingers. Mainliners, some evangelical Christians, and many Catholics are social liberals and progressives. They may disagree on abortion, but they advocate social justice and encourage religious tolerance. Nor can Christianity in this country be understood by the usual liberal/conservative polarity. Some theological liberals are social conservatives, while some theological conservatives will welcome you to worship that is informal, innovative, and contemporary. Fundamentalists aren't nasty people, most are warm and caring, but they often feel threatened in a society that is, for them, far too permissive. Evangelicals are not, as some stereotypes would have it, know-nothings and anti-intellectuals, but often they are among the intellectually and scientifically brightest.

There is no one-size-fits-all for contemporary Christians, nor even two or three sizes or boxes that include all. As a generalization, it seems true that mainline and liberal Christianity has lost clout and prominence in the last half century as many of its adherents have drifted into nonaffiliated and secular status, while evangelical and fundamentalist movements have grown in prominence and organizational skill. They have offered refuge for those who have suffered from personal instability or breakdown of the family and those who are dismayed by cultural changes of the 1960s and '70s. In some respects, George W. Bush both personifies and exemplifies these trends.

While there are beliefs all Christians hold in common, they are often understood and interpreted very differently. There is a similar inner complexity and diversity in most of the world's great religions today. In this new time of pluralism and change, we do well to avoid stereotypes and prejudgments. Today, it's better to approach one another with as much openmindedness and curiosity as we can manage. The long-term challenge for our society in the decades ahead will be to find our way between the extremes of amoral or relativistic forms of liberalism on one hand, and overly prescriptive and intolerant forms of fundamentalism on the other.

# AT THE HINGE
# OF HISTORY:
# POSTMODERNITY

RE WE LIVING at a time of ending or a time of beginning, or both? Many have written of the present era
as shadowed by the sense of an ending, of despair, of
resignation. Still others speak of the emergence of something
new, as yet only dimly perceived. As seems my predilection, I
favor the both/and view of it. To me, ours is a time of cultural
ending and an emergence or a beginning. The particular lens of
experience through which I view this, as well as come to this
conclusion, is that of the more liberal or mainline Protestant
churches. The concurrent eras of American Christendom and
modernity are coming to an end. Some new thing is emerging. Walter Brueggemann, a provocative Old Testament scholar,
once put it this way to a group of pastors: "The world for which
you have been so carefully preparing is being taken away from
you, by the grace of God." That's pretty much the way it goes;
just when you get settled and secure, God intrudes and calls you
to set out again, leaving behind some known world.

The terms *postmodern* and *postmodernity* have been around for
a while now, maybe thirty years say the lexicographers. What in
the world do they mean, and what difference does it all make?

The recently deceased French postmodern philosopher Jacque Derrida provides a clue in his urging that "We become enlightened about the Enlightenment."[23] The ethos and values of the modern world have been so pervasive for so long that we are no more aware of them than fish are, I imagine, aware of water.

Postmodernity's emergence may not be the equivalent of slithering out of the water and onto dry land, but it does mean that we are becoming aware that there are other streams in which to swim. Moreover, we live at one of history's hinge points, when values, scientific worldviews, forms of social organization, technology are all in flux. While few may be aware of this intellectually, almost everyone feels the pull of the riptide and the disorientation of a sea change in their bones and at their nerve endings. We are stroking fast and hard lest we go under, but for all our effort we seem to manage no more than staying afloat and in place. We are stressed and frazzled, and wondering what lies ahead and if we're part of the future picture. For my part, I have a deep interest in the implications of this sea change not only for religion and for the church but for all areas of life. A new era is emerging not only because of new ideas, of course, but due to new technologies, new science, and new forms of social organization: the television, computer, and Internet; the new physics and biology; the global economy; and revolution in military affairs spurred by technology and non-state combatants; these are both symptoms and causes of an emerging postmodern world.

Some historians date the beginning of the modern era as early as 1500 and the emergence of the Renaissance. More often people peg modernity around 1648, the year that the Treaty of Westphalia ended the devastating Thirty Years' War, which had raged across Europe since 1618. Others mark modernity's beginning in the early 1700s. There's never any precise dating of such things because it's only interpretation. But the changes are real nonetheless and they have enormous consequences. I grew up in the world of modernity, but now I live in a post-modern world. When exactly it shifted I can't tell you, but that it has I am sure.

The world of my childhood and youth, the world of modernity, was ruled by at least five core values: rationality, optimism, universality, objectivity, and trust in an all-embracing narrative. As children of the Enlightenment, we had tremendous trust in reason and in our capacity to figure everything out by rational means. I recall my own high-rationalist phase. I was a junior in college when I became enamored (a little late, thought my parents) of study and critical thought. I was completely confident that if only we put our minds to it we could figure everything out, life would make sense, and we would live happily ever after. I expressed this confidence in a letter to my younger sister, explaining to her that "If you will just think, think critically, you can make sense of everything and work it all out." She never responded to that letter, which I take as a sign of her graciousness!

Postmoderns have a good deal less confidence in reason and rationality, at least as the sole means of knowing, or as a means to find solutions to all our problems. Today people are exploring different ways of knowing: intuition, emotional intelligence, embodied knowledge, sensory awareness, and mystical experience, to name just a few. In the mail today I received an invitation to group devoted to "reading" our dreams. Reason remains a powerful tool and an important human faculty, but it is no longer the undisputed lord and master. Indeed, the overly rational are now viewed as limited and out of touch. "Don't just talk out of your head," I've heard people complain, "speak to us from your heart!"

One of the ways this played out in the world of faith and religion can be illustrated by *The Jefferson Bible*. An Enlightenment man, a rationalist, and a deist, Thomas Jefferson created his own version of the New Testament (the Old Testament was too primitive for a self-respecting modern to bother with). Taking scissors and paste to the sacred writings (itself an audacious thing to do), Jefferson snipped out the miracles one by one, and excised the passages that mentioned supernatural elements. The end product is, needless to say, a small book. What was left was morality, moral teachings, and Jesus the teacher, which is about the best a strict modernist can hope for. Jefferson's Bible illustrates what happens when reason eclipses revelation, when rationality is the sole criteria of admissibility to the canon. Religion is reduced to a moral code, which is of course, part of any religion, but hardly all of it. In fact, morality without spirituality is works without grace. That is, it is all about what we should do (morality), but little about what God, divine powers, grace (spirituality) has done. Modernity turned Christianity, a religion of grace, into a religion of good works and achievement. I don't mean, of course, that Jefferson himself did this. I do mean that the attempt to accommodate Christianity to modernity did. Spirituality, with its faith in the miraculous and mysterious, was lost or repressed. The end result was thin fare, a moral code without transformative power. It is religion as obligation but lacking much in the way of motivation or motivating power.

Not only did modernity prize reason the way that a toddler who has just learned to walk prizes that new skill, the intoxication with reason led to a spirit of general and enthusiastic optimism. Many believed it was only a matter of time before reason, expressed through its practical handmaid, technology, would uncover solutions to all of humanity's problems. Science and technology would enable us to gain control over the vicissitudes of nature and to free ourselves from our various forms of social bondage. "Better living through chemistry," proclaimed General Electric. The future will be one of leisure, creativity, ease, and enjoyment, proclaimed various World's Fair exhibits of the modern era. Every man and every woman would be a member of the new landed gentry of modernity, an aristocracy born of technology. In the latter part of the twentieth century most Americans discovered themselves working longer hours and harder than ever. Something must have been off in the calculation of modernity's imminent utopia.

Postmoderns tend not to be optimists. They are skeptics, even pessimists about the great promises of controlling nature and ushering in either a secular utopia or the Kingdom of God on earth through reason, science, and education. I remember the eruption of Mount St. Helens in Washington State in 1980. The eruption was greeted with a sense of shock and disbelief, as if to say, "What's this? What's going on here? Listen, we're modern people, this is the First World, we don't do volcanoes. That's Third World stuff. We've got nature under control!" Well, maybe not. Twenty-five years later, when St. Helens signaled the possibility of another eruption, the reaction was different, more postmodern. Hundreds of people began making what can only be described as pilgrimages to view nature's wonder and power. The hubris of controlling nature had given way to awe and wonder.

As moderns, we not only thought we could control nature, we thought we could solve our most vexing social problems if we simply put our best minds to it. Poverty, racism, sexism would be solved through "consciousness raising" and well-timed programmatic interventions. This optimism died in Vietnam, where our best minds couldn't figure out how to win the war. It died on the streets and in the boardrooms of Los Angeles, Detroit, and Washington, D.C., where poverty and racism proved to have considerable staying power. We could, and should, work for greater justice. We could, and should, work to ameliorate human suffering, but we began to suspect that the world's problems would not be fixed as if the world were a machine in need of a tune-up. Moreover, human sin, selfishness, and self-deception will not be educated or legislated out of existence.

In embracing the optimistic spirit of modernity, Christianity in its modern and liberal versions tended to overlook sin. So much so that Karl Menninger famously asked, "Whatever Became of Sin?" in his 1974 book by that title. Truth to tell, Christianity was never all that optimistic, at least about us humans. The church generally believes humans are, at best, a mixed bag: children of God and yet creatures of dust. We are made of marble and mud, one foot on earth and one foot in heaven. However we choose to explain or understand it, we are forever deceiving ourselves about ourselves, forever distorting life, and inclined to make ourselves the center of things. In trying to catch the spirit of a more optimistic modern age, Christianity became, ironically, less realistic; it hit the delete key on its core understanding of sin and the tragic dimension of life.

Another characteristic of the modern era was its love of universals and universality. My wife's grandparents came to the United States from Czechoslovakia and Spain. They spoke Czech and Spanish in their homes and to their children because, at least initially, that's all they knew how to speak. By the time my wife and her siblings were growing up the languages of the old country were not taught to them. "We shall become Americans" was the sentiment and goal of parents of the modern era. They would become part of the great American melting pot, where particularity is melted away and we become a new person, an American. That's hardly all bad, of course, just as other values of modernity—reason and optimism—have much to be said on their behalf. Modern America was a new nation and joining the melting pot had its value. Still, the bias toward universality had its costs and was, in some ways, an illusion. There is no universal human, free of context and history. Moreover, this universality tended to discredit certain values and social practices as illegitimate. There was one way to be human.

But not for postmoderns, who are in love with the unique and the unusual, and who celebrate the distinctive flavor of the regional and the local. People are now studying the languages and cultures that earlier generations had been happier to forget. People search almost frantically at times for roots and connection. Some of this is certainly fashion and trend, but at a deeper level it signals that we are creatures shaped by particular contexts, histories, stories, and languages. Fewer speak of universal truth, truth for all times and places.

This shift is also reflected in the world of faith and Christianity by the move in the postmodern period away from abstractions and theological propositions to stories and narrative. For a time in the modern era, Christianity had been presented as a set of universal and timeless truths. Moreover, Christianity was presented as the final and ultimate religion, which was in line with modernist notions of progress; other religions were considered only as preparatory steps and stages. The notion of the Bible as a story, a great narrative, had been largely lost. To be sure there are timeless truths and moral values, but they tend to come wrapped up in story and narrative, in context and in community. In the postmodern period story, narrative, ritual, and sacrament are all enjoying a renaissance.

Closely related to the turn toward universality was modernity's embrace of the idea and ideal of objectivity. Through reason and by commitment to universal truths, moderns believed they could be completely objective. We could rise above history's vicissitudes and transcend our own limitations. Objectivity, like the rest, has its real value, and we will be impoverished if we jettison all notions of balance and fairness. But absolute objectivity is an illusion. We can strive to be fair. We can listen to different perspectives and consider opposing viewpoints. We can try to be aware of our own prejudices and our bias. But can we be truly and completely objective? It turns out that the interviewer affects the interview, the researcher shapes the research, and the scientist influences the experiment.

For a time in the heyday of modernity there was the view, as mentioned above, that other religions could be appreciated as preliminary steps, preparatory stages, to the final and true religion, which was, surprise, our own. This was considered a modern and objective truth, one marvelously adept at tidying up the mess of human life. Steps, stages, evolution—it all fits in. The only problem was that it didn't all fit together, and other faiths did not appreciate being relegated to the status of warm-up acts. One could see somewhat the same notion at work in cultures and nations, and human history itself. The modern West, Christian and American, was considered the culmination of human history, of human learning and culture: we believed we held the objective and universal truth. Well, maybe not. Today we live in a postmodern world of many points of view and worldviews—sometimes they complement each other, sometimes they compete with one another. Of course, this is not without problems of its own, but no longer can modernists insist that their viewpoint is the objective and universal one.

A final characteristic of modernity was its wonderful confidence in the big story and the grand narrative. It is the idea, the narrative, that through reason and its application in science, education, and technology, we human beings will plumb the depths and solve the mysteries, which are no longer mysteries at all so much as problems awaiting solution. We will gain the answers and achieve control. Postmoderns tend not to buy into this grand narrative. They are agnostics when it comes to big stories that define what it means to be human in all times and places. Their narratives are smaller stories, more local and particular ventures.

In the end, Christianity, like all religions, is a meta narrative, a big story. Christians cannot embrace, at least without some careful nuances, the relativity of postmodernism. But we can take steps toward respecting and appreciating the wisdom of other faiths, traditions, and cultures, as well as learning to share our own in a way that encourages dialogue.

A friend, Stan Grenz, who is a theologian, pointed out that the famed television series *Star Trek* illustrates the shift from modernity to postmodernity. Remember the original *Star Trek* show? Spock was the ideal of the modernist perspective: the eminently rational man. He was not burdened by emotions. He was completely rational, and when the going got tough, Spock was the go-to guy. And on that original 1960s voyage, the crew of the ship was assembled from many nations, but blended into one universal spirit and venture. Ethnic identities were overcome and cast aside in pursuit of the great adventure of obtaining objective knowledge of the universe and of exploring the "final frontier" of space.

Let's fast-forward to the late-1980s version of *Star Trek: The Next Generation*. An android named Data has assumed Spock's role. Like Spock, Data is eminently rational. But unlike Spock, Data wants more—he wants to be human, he wants to feel and to have emotions. Data's rational skills are balanced by those of others, including a woman, Counselor Troi, who is gifted with the ability to read the feelings and emotions of others. Also, the makeup of the crew of the *Enterprise* reflects the postmodern perspective: it is not limited to humans of various nations on earth; it comprises varied species from throughout the universe. In a postmodern sensibility, universality is broader and more inclusive, and we humans are not the only advanced intelligence in the cosmos. And even the quest has changed. It is no longer the quest of humankind alone, but of humankind in partnership with the universe to explore the mysteries of space and life itself. It is an unfinished venture with no end in sight because we stand not on the cusp of the final frontier but a whole new universe. In the different iterations of this television show, we can see ourselves groping to understand the shift from modernity to some strange new postmodern world.

To become enlightened about the Enlightenment, as Derrida urged us, means that the values of modernity need not be privileged or enjoy the taken-for-granted status that has so long been true. They too are subject to critique. But this is not to say that rationality, optimism, universality, objectivity, and modernity's grand narrative about the human adventure are now relegated to history's scrap heap. It's not nearly that easy or that simple. Modernity's characteristics, values, and accomplishments continue to have their positive aspects, as well as their negative ones.

"The times," as that great philosopher Bob Dylan said, "they are a-changin'." In terms of my specific experience within mainline and liberal Christianity, the changes mean a huge challenge. We, mainline Christians, opened our arms to modernity and tried to adjust Christianity to the modern world. In contrast, fundamentalists circled the wagons against modernity and its values, which they perceived as a threat. In between the modernity-embracing liberals and the modernity-averse fundamentalists, Christians in the evangelical, charismatic, and Catholic branches made a more qualified acceptance of modernity. Among the challenges before the mainline, liberal Christianity is sorting out which of our values are Christian and which are modern, as well as learning to be the church in a postmodern time.

These times are heady and nerve-wracking, full of danger and rich in opportunity for all of us, not just in the religious world but in every world. The ways of doing things in the modern era are in flux and up for grabs in every walk of life: in education and science, in the arts and religion, in medicine and law, in social organization and communication, in military and leadership, and many others. It is scary and wonderful, exciting and confusing.

Amid these challenges we need to be patient with one another as well as with ourselves. We must try to learn from each other. We need to sort out what is precious from what is expendable. We must learn from our past without being held captive to it. Instead of building fences and walls to separate ourselves from others, we need to build bridges and overpasses. Bridges to cross over to others, and overpasses so that we can get over some of the accumulated detritus and useless baggage that has built up and keeps us separate. One world is passing away and a new one is emerging, but none of us see that new one clearly or completely yet. While we try to negotiate this sea change, we will need all hands on deck and as much help as we can get.

# ENDNOTES

**PART ONE**

1. Flannery O'Connor, quoted in Peter S. Hawkins, *The Language of Grace* (New York: Seabury Classics, 2004), p. 21.

2. John Calvin, *Commentary on the Book of Psalms*, tr. J. Anderson (Grand Rapids: Eerdmans Publishing, 1949), p. xl.

3. Walker Percy, *The Second Coming* (New York: Farrer, Straus & Giroux, 1980), p. 272.

4. Ronald A. Heifetz and Marty Linsky, *Leadership on the Line* (Boston: Harvard Business School Press, 2002), p. 12.

5. Belden Lane, *Landscapes of the Sacred* (New York: Paulist Press, 1988), p. 21.

6. Ibid., p. 21.

7. Belden Lane, quoted in Constance Fitzgerald, O. C. D., "Impasse and Dark Night," *Living with Apocalypse* (New York: Harper and Row, 1984), p. 96.

8. Ernest Hemingway, *A Farewell to Arms* (New York: Charles Scribner's Sons, 1929).

9. Barbara Brown Taylor, "Life Giving Fear," *Home by Another Way* (Cambridge: Cowley Publications, 1999).

10. Dietrich Bonhoeffer, *Letters and Papers from Prison* (New York: Macmillan, 1972), p. 361.

11. Thomas Merton, quoted in Robert Benson, *Living Prayer* (New York: Putnam, 1998), p. 1.

12. Black Elk, quoted in Richard Kehl, *Silver Departures* (La Jolla, CA: The Green Tiger Press, 1983), p. 8.

## PART TWO

1   Wendell Berry, *The Gift of the Good Land* (New York: North Point Press, 1982), p. 159.

2   Rabbi Edwin Friedman, *Generation to Generation: Family Process in Church and Synagogue* (New York: The Guildford Press, 1985), p. 2.

3   Berry, *Good Land*, p. 159.

4   Alvin Rosenfeld, *Hyper-Parenting: Are You Hurting Your Child by Trying Too Hard?* Quote is from Web site, www.hyperparenting. com.

5   Michael Sandel, "The Case Against Perfection: What's Wrong with Designer Children, Bionic Athletes, and Genetic Engineering," *The Atlantic Monthly* 293, no. 3 (2004).

6   Erik H. Erikson, *Childhood and Society* (New York: W. W. Norton, 1963), p. 247.

7   Amanda Paulson, "Busy Children: Quick! Is Johnny Signed Up for Daydreaming?" *Christian Science Monitor*, September 8, 2004, pp. 1, 10.

8   Nathaniel Hawthorne, *The House of Seven Gables* (New York: Signet Classics, 1981), p. 42.

9   Parker Palmer, *The Company of Strangers: Christians and the Renewal of America's Public Life* (New York: Crossroad, 1983), p. 17.

10  Renita J. Weems, "Song of Songs," *New Interpreter's Bible* (Nashville: Abingdon, 1997), p. 381.

## PART THREE

1   Jaroslav Pelikan, *The Melody of Theology: A Philosophical Dictionary* (Cambridge: Harvard University Press, 1988), p. 252.

2   John W. Gardner, *On Leadership* (New York: The Free Press, 1993).

3   Ibid., p. 113.

4   William Sloane Coffin, *Credo* (Louisville: Westminster John Knox Press, 2004), p. 113.

5   Gregg Easterbrook, *The Progress Paradox: How Life Gets Better While People Feel Worse* (New York: Random House, 2003), p. 230.

6   Robert Emmons in Easterbrook, *Progress Paradox*, p. 238.

7   Easterbrook, *Progress Paradox*, p. 235.

8   Frederick Buechner, *Wishful Thinking: A Theological ABC* (New York: Harper and Row, 1973), p. 2.

9   Deborah Tannen, *The Argument Culture* (New York: Random House, 1998), p. 3.

10  Ibid., p. 4.

11  Daniel Kemmis, *The Good City and the Good Life* (Boston: Houghton Mifflin, 1995), p. 9.

12  Ibid., p. 9.

13  John Winthrop, in Gerald N. Grob and Robert N. Beck, ed., *American Ideas* (New York: Free Press, 1963), p. 37.

14  Benjamin DeMott, *The Trouble with Friendship: Why Americans Can't Think Straight About Race*, quoted in Willimon, "Why We All Can't Just Get Along," *Theology Today* 54, no. 4 (January 1997), p. 487.

15  William H. Willimon, "Why We All Can't Just Get Along," *Theology Today* 54, no. 4 (January 1997), p. 489.

16  John Hope Franklin, *The Color Line: Legacy for the Twenty-first Century* (Columbia: University of Missouri Press, 1993), p. 74.

17  Paul Tillich, *The Shaking of the Foundations* (New York: Charles Scribner's Sons, 1948), p. 1.

18  Diana Butler Bass, *Broken We Kneel: Reflections on Faith and Citizenship* (San Francisco: Jossey-Bass, 2004), p. 62.

19  Ibid., p. 68.

20  Ibid., p. 67.

21  Jean Bethke Elshtain, *Just War Against Terror* (New York: Basic Books, 2003) pp. 112–113.

22  Leslie Marmon Silko, *Ceremony* (New York: Penguin, 1977), p. 2.

23  Jacques Derrida, quoted in Brian D. McLaren, *The Church on the Other Side* (Grand Rapids: Zondervan, 1998), p. 190.

# ABOUT THE AUTHOR

A Northwest native by birth, **Anthony B. Robinson** also spent formative years on the east coast. As a pastor he has had a chance to study life close up. The congregations he has served include churches that are rural and urban, small and large, multi-cultural and predominantly Anglo. As an author, he has had the opportunity to step back and get a larger perspective. He is the author of eight books, including the bestselling *Transforming Congregational Culture* (Eerdmans, 2003), and many articles. He writes a regular opinion column for the editorial pages of the *Seattle Post-Intelligencer.* He lives in Seattle with his wife, Linda, who works as a school principal. They have three children. Gardening, backpacking, kayaking, and wine are things he enjoys.

# ABOUT THE AUTHOR

A Northwest native by birth, **Anthony B. Robinson** also spent formative years on the east coast. As a pastor he has had a chance to study life close up. The congregations he has served include churches that are rural and urban, small and large, multi-cultural and predominantly Anglo. As an author, he has had the opportunity to step back and get a larger perspective. He is the author of eight books, including the best-selling *Transforming Congregational Culture* (Eerdmans, 2003), and many articles. He writes a regular opinion column for the editorial pages of the *Seattle Post-Intelligencer.* He lives in Seattle with his wife, Linda, who works as a school principal. They have three children. Gardening, backpacking, kayaking, and wine are things he enjoys.